"Many people ‡   r
coaching. Then ⌐   l
is the 'secret weapon' for a great experience. It s easy and rewarding to do-it-yourself. A few minutes a day gives me performance under my feet, whether I'm skiing Alpine, Telemark, back-country or groomed-track cross-country."

— Ned Gillette
Adventure Skier

"When I picked up this book I expected a painful read through something like the dry textbooks of my youth. How else might a book like this read?

"From the very first page it was clear that the authors knew how to do better. *Waxing and Care of Skis and Snowboards* has been carefully written, wonderfully edited and nicely organized to make using it and yes, reading it, a pleasure. A clean and concise introduction is followed by a well organized, comprehensive reference section and a good index designed to make the book useful for beginning skiers and skilled repair shop employees alike.

"I like its focus on practicality, urging the recreational reader to delve into its details only as far as necessary to help make sliding on snow fun. And a recreational reader can certainly get to the heart of the matter in a hurry with this book.

"So too can a professional technician or racing coach who needs a comprehensive reference. Hats off to Brady and Torgersen for a fine effort. *Waxing and Care of Skis and Snowboards* will have a home in my reference library."

— Craig Sabina
President, Summit Projects

"Torgersen and Brady make the science of waxing easy to understand and with historical detail make the wax culture live. The difference between a great and a so so day of gliding on snow is in this book."

— Bob Woodward
Products Editor, Snow Country Magazine

Waxing and Care of Skis and Snowboards

Michael Brady

Leif Torgersen

WILDERNESS PRESS
BERKELEY

Library of Congress Card Number 96-19830
ISBN 0-89997-199-7

Manufactured in the United States of America

Published by Wilderness Press
              2440 Bancroft Way
              Berkeley, CA 94704
              (800) 443-7227
              FAX (510) 548-1355

              Write, call or fax us for a free catalog

Library of Congress Cataloging-in-Publication Data

Brady, M. Michael.
    Waxing and care of skis and snowboards / Michael Brady and Leif
Torgersen. — 1st ed.
        p.   cm.
    Includes index.
    ISBN 0-89997-199-7
    1. Ski waxing. 2. Skis and skiing—Equipment and supplies—
    Maintenance and repair. 3. Snowboards—Maintenance and repair.
    I. Torgersen, Leif. II. Title.
    GV855.5.W39B73 1996
    796.93—dc20   96-19830
                                                           CIP

CONTENTS

HOW TO USE THIS BOOK

Doubtless, few will read this book like a novel, from cover to cover. Equally doubtless, no two skiers or snowboarders are equally proficient or equally experienced. So this book is structured to provide ready access to information on waxing, so you, the reader, can glean the details that best suit your needs. The book has three sections.

The Way is an overview of waxing today and a guide to how to suit waxing to your needs.

The **Reference** is an encyclopedia of the topics that comprise waxing, in alphabetical order.

The **Index** is an alphabetical reference to the entire book.

If you are an experienced skier or snowboarder, you probably will seek information on specific topics. Look them up in the index, and read the pages listed.

If you are new to skiing or snowboarding and wish to learn the basics of waxing, we recommend that you read The Way, Applying Wax, Choosing Waxes, Glide Waxes (and Grip Waxes if you are a classical cross-country skier), Easy Waxing, and Safety.

If your capabilities and needs place you between those two extremes, you probably will want to read up on selected topics in the Reference section.

Above all, enjoy your skiing or snowboarding. That's the ultimate purpose of the art and science of waxing.

Michael Brady
Leif Torgersen

About the photos of waxing techniques

The glide waxing photos show only Alpine skis or cross-country skis, but the techniques shown apply to all skis and snowboards. Likewise, some steps are the same in all procedures, such as melting waxes against the warm sole of an iron, which is done in the same way, regardless of whether bases are being prepared, waxed for the day or cleaned. Consequently, some photos are repeated, to underscore the similarities of the steps of the various waxing techniques.

There are two exceptions to this uniformity. Edge filing is done only on Alpine skis, Telemark skis, and snowboards, so the techniques of it are shown on an Alpine ski. Likewise, grip waxing is done only for classical cross-country skiing, so its techniques are shown on a cross-country ski.

The photos are close-ups of the details that you should concentrate on in performing the various techniques. Most of the photos show a ski clamped horizontally, base up, as skis and snowboards should be for thorough waxing. The six photos of Easy Waxing show it as it is most often done: ski upright, as you hold it in one hand, tail down on the floor, while waxing its base with the other hand.

READ THIS

The methods and materials discussed in this book serve their purpose when properly used. If you have any doubt about using them, seek professional advice. The authors and the publisher specifically disclaim responsibility for injury or damage resulting from improper use of these methods and materials.

THE WAY

The gliding of skis and sled runners on different snows is an extremely difficult subject.
Fridtjof Nansen, Arctic explorer, 1930.

Explorer Nansen could not have known it then, but his statement was to have lasting impact. Modern skis and waxes have eased the problems that concerned him, and snow science has provided a better understanding of nature's most fickle material. The complexity remains, but the ways of coping with it have become user-friendly. That's what this book is about.

Three generations; American roots

The world's first commercial ski wax was *Sierra Lightning*, which the California gold rush miners of the 1860s brewed for their downhill ski races. That product fostered the first generation of ski waxing, during which natural compounds were put on wood skis. Mixing was mostly by hand, compounds were found by trial and error, and wax-base performance was correspondingly spotty.

That era lasted some 80 years. Then, in the late 1940s, the first ski waxes compounded of synthetic materials were made and marketed. They contained waxes, resins, and rubbers related to those in industrial lubricants and motor fuels. That triggered the industrial-scale production of ski waxes. Skis followed suit, in the mid 1950s through mid 1970s, as synthetic materials replaced the natural materials formerly used. By the late 1970s, the second generation was in full flower. Synthetics ruled the roost, and waxed-base performance was dependable, thanks to consistent compounding. But waxing remained the art of applying coatings to bases.

The pace of technology quickened; the second generation lasted less than half as long as the first. By the late 1980s, waxes containing super-slick fluorocarbons, the compounds snow scientists had long sought, were available in shops. Glide was recognized as the common denominator for all movement on snow - on Alpine skis, Telemark skis, jumping skis, cross-country skis and snowboards - and this recognition brought about universal approaches to glide waxing. The grip of classical cross-country skiing then was seen as a case of reduced glide requiring waxes and techniques dedicated to the purpose. Snow scientists neatly tied all these matters into theories that explained the actions of skis or snowboards moving on snow in terms of an intervening interface. That's where we are now: *glide* is the keyword, and *waxing* means the unified activity of working, or "finishing," bases and applying waxes to match one side of the interface with the underlying snow surface.

Snow reigns

Despite an allure that appeals in photography, painting and poetry, snow is one of nature's more variable materials. The principal reason is that snow comprises tiny ice crystals which are formed in the atmosphere and thereafter are continually changing. The understanding of this complexity also has firm American roots.

In 1904, two scientists independently evolved breakthrough theories of raindrop formation. One was Wilson Bentley (1865-1931), a self-educated farmer who lived his entire life in the village of Jericho, Vermont. The other was Phillipp Eduard Anton Lenard (1862-1947), a professor of physics at Heidelberg, Germany. Bentley went on to pioneer the microphotography of snow crystals and to delight audiences with his findings. Lenard went on to be awarded the 1905 Nobel Prize in Physics and to have a brilliant academic career.

Lenard's eminent scientific credentials underscore the complexity of the meteorological phenomena that he studied. Bently may well have been equally gifted in probing that complexity. And thanks to the foresight of William J. Humphreys, then chief physicist for the US Weather Bureau, the best of Bentley's snow-crystal microphotographs were collected and published by McGraw-Hill, just a few weeks before Bentley's death in 1931. Under the simple title *Snow Crystals*, Humphreys' collection of Bentley's work became a classic of snow science as well as a tribute to the art of nature. Fortunately, an unabridged facsimile of it, first released in 1962 by Dover Publications, is still available, ISBN 0-486-20287-9, $15.95, paperback. A similar edition, aimed at children, 5th grade and up, has been released by Peter Smith, ISBN 0-8446-1660-5, $24.95.

As soon as snow falls on the ground, it begins to age and change. Subsequent weather determines the speed and nature of the changes. So today's snow conditions depend both on today's weather and on the prevailing meteorological history since the snow fell. Weather is the major, but not the only, factor affecting snow conditions. Pure snow hasn't changed since the time of Bentley and Lenard, but the snows of snow sports differ from the pure stuff. First, snow purity has diminished through the years, due to contamination by airborne pollutants. Second, almost all ski areas use grooming machines and, in some cases, chemicals that alter snow on the ground to upgrade it for skiing and snowboarding. Finally, the globe is getting warmer: the average surface temperature of the Earth rose 1.5°F from 1860 through 1995; about half the increase came after 1950, just as skiing and then snowboarding grew rapidly worldwide. Because global warming produces erratic winter weather, ski areas increasingly rely on artificial snow. Because it usually is made from local water found on or under the ground, artificial snow differs from the natural stuff.

Define and prevail

Modern waxing provides an arsenal of techniques to match various snow conditions. That's what the rest of this book is about. For any given snow condition, the more extensive waxing techniques usually result in the higher performance on snow. But returns diminish as waxing effort increases: spending twice as long waxing doesn't double final performance on snow. A racer, or a racer's technician, may spend an extra hour for the hopeful gain of a few hundredths of a second in a downhill race. But for a recreational Alpine skier, that hour isn't worth the effort, as outright speed isn't the object in a day of skiing.

So the best waxing techniques are those that best suit your needs. Do you, for instance, ski or snowboard infrequently or regularly, for recreation or as a profession, such as instructing or ski patrolling? Or do you race? Answers to questions such as these define your waxing needs and enable you to gain the greatest performance dividend for your time spent waxing. There are two major categories:

Easy: you are a recreational skier or a recreational skiing professional. Speed is not your prime goal, but you seek skiing ease. The time you spend waxing depends on how seriously you take your skiing or snowboarding.

Racing: you are a competitor interested in ultimate ski performance. Consequently, you (or your technician) will spend the time required for the ultimate of waxing techniques.

Reference

APPLYING WAX

Wax indoors whenever possible. It's more comfortable than standing outside, and wax goes on and sticks better when both wax and base are at indoor temperatures. Likewise, try always to work on a horizontal base, of a ski held in waxing vises or a waxing horse, or of a snowboard held by suction-cup clamps. A stable surface speeds and eases work.

Always start with a clean, dry pair of skis or a clean, dry snowboard. Wax doesn't stick to dirt or water. If you have waxed wrongly for the day's snow, remove the old wax and clean bases before rewaxing (see **Cleaning bases**).

The best way to apply wax is that which best suits your needs, your skis or board, and the wax applied. If you are a recreational skier or snowboarder, you most likely prefer speed and ease in waxing. See **Easy waxing** for a guide as how to do it with as little as possible. If performance is your goal, or if you are a racer, you probably will spend more time to achieve the results that accurate waxing affords. You may use some or all of the techniques of glide waxing and, if you are a classical cross-country skier, grip waxing as well.

Glide waxes - four ways, one for each form

Glide waxes come in four forms: solid blocks, pastes, liquids, and powders (see **Glide waxes** for further details). Hot waxing with solid blocks is the backbone waxing technique for racing and high-performance recreational skiing and snowboarding. But it is time-consuming and must be done indoors, usually in a room dedicated to waxing. So most recreational skiers and snowboarders will prefer the convenience and speed of waxing with pastes or liquids. Powders are high-tech, and accordingly expensive, materials intended to boost the performance of hot-waxed bases. They are usually used only in racing.

Hot waxing with solid blocks

Heating bonds a glide wax to a base better than any other method, because the molten wax and warmed base plastic actually mix slightly, in a manner chemists call a *solution*. The base plastic itself is not porous, as is often popularly assumed in explanations of its ability to hold wax. If it were, it would also act like a sponge and absorb water. It doesn't, because it is *hydrophobic*: it repels water. Heat is the catalyst that brews the wax-plastic solution, bonding the wax to the base.

Start preparing a base with the ski or board horizontal and firmly clamped, base up. Work with a small block of glide wax, as it's easier to handle than a large block. The 20 gr. (0.7 oz) blocks broken off at the indentations on larger blocks are ideal.

Melt the wax onto the base with an iron, set to 100° to 130°C (212° to 266°F), or *low* to *medium* on an ordinary household electric iron. Special waxing irons, available from wax manufacturers, usually have settings indexed to the waxes applied. If you use a block iron heated in a torch flame or heat gun air stream, heat it to the point where wax touched to it melts and just begins to smoke. Hold the corner of the iron just above the base, press the wax against the iron so it melts, and drip molten wax down on the base, in two long strips on a ski or in several long strips on a snowboard.

Iron the wax into the base, using the iron flat on the base. Keep it moving, to prevent overheating. As shown in the graph, the penetration of wax into the base depends on the temperature

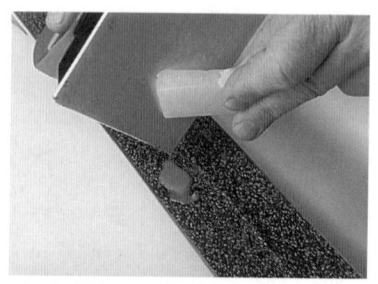

Start glide waxing by melting wax onto base with warm iron

Iron wax in

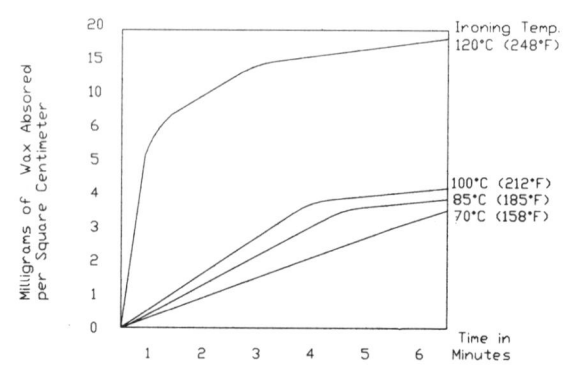

Wax absorption in base increases with heating time

of the iron and how long you iron.

Let the base cool at room temperature until the wax has hardened, which usually takes 20 to 30 minutes.

Scrape the wax on the base to an thin, smooth layer, using a plastic scraper. If the base has a tracking groove, remove the excess wax from it with a round, dull object, such as the corner of a groove scraper or of a klister spreader paddle.

Brush in the longitudinal direction, until you see the underlying structure of the base. Use a nylon-bristle waxing brush for softer glide waxes (for "warmer" snows) and a mixed-fiber-bristle waxing brush for harder glide waxes (for colder snows). Always finish with a softer nylon-bristle brush, to polish the surface.

Paste waxing

Squeeze the tube to extrude strips of paste on the base, or use a small plastic spatula to apply it from a can. Spread it evenly over the base, using a cloth or wiping tissue. Let it dry for the period of time recommended in its instructions, usually about 10 to 15 minutes at room temperature. Then polish it with a cork for best results.

Scrape wax to a thin, smooth layer

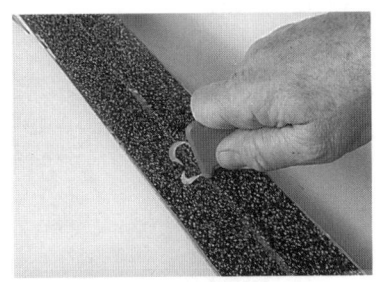

If the base has a tracking groove, remove excess cooled wax from it

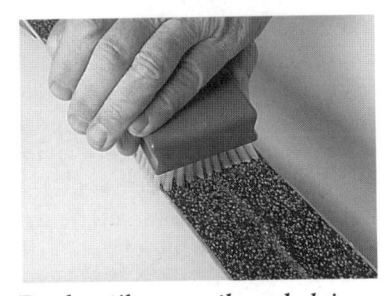

Brush until you see the underlying structure of the base

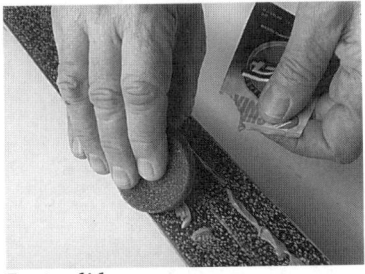

Paste glide wax

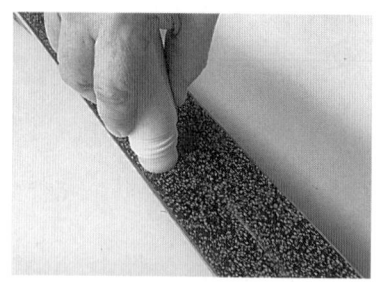

Liquid glide waxing, swab container shown

Liquid waxing

Swab, brush or spray the liquid on the base, depending on its type - fluid, aerosol or pump spray - and let it dry for the period of time recommended in its instructions, usually about 5 to 10 minutes at room temperature. Then polish it with a cork for best results.

Powder booster waxing

A fluorocarbon powder acts as a booster to improve the glide of a hot-waxed base. Start with the ski or board horizontal and firmly clamped, base up. Sprinkle the powder on the entire glide-waxed area of the base, as if sparingly but thoroughly salting a breakfast egg. Then blend and bond the powder into the underlying glide wax. You can do that hot or cold, depending on the equipment on hand, the time you have available, and your own skills as a waxer.

Hot blending and bonding starts as does the ironing step of hot waxing. With the iron temperature set at about 120°C (248°F), move it along the base, from tip to tail, in one steady stroke, or several strokes to completely cover the base of a snowboard (but never twice over the same area). That's all you need do to melt the powder into the underlying wax. A visual check is the best way to see if you have done it right. As you move the iron along the base, watch for small, telltale *scintillations* - sparks, like those given off by a fireworks sparkler, of the kind kids wave on the 4th of July. Move the iron just fast enough so the sparks just die out. Let the base cool for about 15 minutes at room temperature,

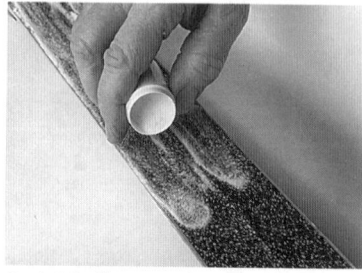

Sprinkle fluorocarbon powder on

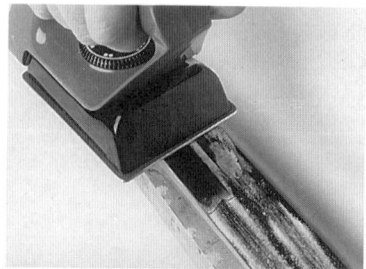

Iron in powder; watch for small sparks

and then brush it to remove the even gloss left by the iron, first with a stiffer mixed-fiber-bristle brush, and then with a softer nylon-bristle brush.

Cork powder firmly to blend and bond it to the underlying wax

Brush after corking powder

Cold blending and bonding substitutes the mechanical work of a cork for the heat of an iron. Cork with secure, strong strokes, to work the powder into the underlying wax, until you no longer can see the individual powder wax particles. Then brush the base with a nylon-bristle brush.

Grip waxing for classical cross-country

Grip waxing involves applying either a *hard wax* or a *klister* (see **Grip waxes**) to the **Kick zone** of the base in performance waxing or over the entire base in **Easy waxing**.

Hard waxes: All dry-snow waxes and some wet-snow waxes of two-wax **Easy waxing** sets come in foil cans, so start by peeling off a strip of foil, about 1/4 in. broad, to expose the wax. Use a sharp object, such as the corner of a ski scraper, to start the peel. A thumbnail may do the job if the can is made of a soft aluminum alloy or plastic, but if it is made of tougher metal, the can will probably win over your thumbnail and send you running for the first-aid kit.

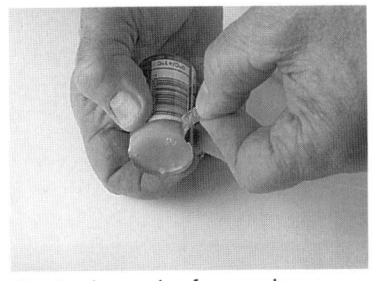

Start grip waxing by opening a hard wax can

Apply the wax by holding the can at an angle to the base, as if you were writing with chalk on a blackboard, and crayon the wax on in short, rapid strokes. Don't wax the tracking groove in the center of the base. It provides no grip if waxed, and can fill

with wax, which will cause the
ski to *yaw* or "swim" when
gliding. Then smooth and
bond the wax to the base. You
can do that hot or cold, depending on the performance
you seek, the equipment on
hand, the time you have available, and your own skills as a
waxer.

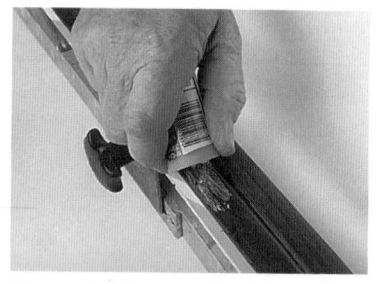

Crayon hard wax out using long, even strokes

Hot smoothing and bond-
ing gives the most durable bond. With the ski clamped horizontal, base up, iron the wax in. Use an iron with its thermostat set
at about 100°C (212°F), or *low* on an ordinary household electric
iron. Iron back and forth until the all the wax appears molten.
Then let the wax cool, for about 15 to 20 minutes at room temperature. Cork out the cooled wax until it shines. Add more layers if you wish, corking each out. Many thin layers are always
better than few thick layers. But don't warm in the second and
subsequent layers. If you do so, you create a single, thick layer,
which defeats the purpose of multiple layers.

Cold smoothing and bonding is quicker than hot smoothing
and bonding and, if done well, gives almost as good a bond to
the base. Cork out the wax using long, even strokes. Continue
corking until the wax appears warmed on its surface. Let it cool
for a few minutes before applying subsequent layers.

Base binders are special waxes intended to bind hard waxes
to a ski base, for greater durability on abrasive snows. Never put
base binder on the glide zones of the base, as it can slow glide.
Remember: **Stick under grip, slide under glide!**

There are two types of base binder: hard wax, like a hard grip
wax, and spray. Apply hard base binder to the clean kick zone of
the base and warm it in thor-
oughly with an iron. Let it cool
to room temperature. Resist the
temptation to set the skis outside to speed cooling. Just as
windows fog up when a car
parked in a warm garage is
driven out into the cold, warm
base wax will collect moisture
from the outside air. As the
wax cools, the moisture freezes

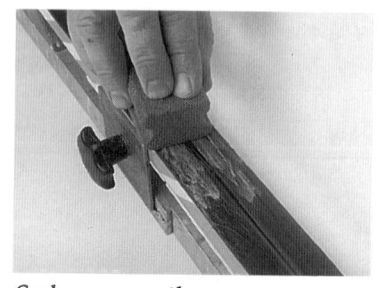

Cork wax smooth

to become small ice crystals. Because wax won't stick to ice, that destroys the effect of the base wax.

After the base wax has cooled, cork it out to a thin, transparent layer. Keep a separate cork for the purpose (label its end with a marking pen), as base binder picked up by the cork can contaminate and slow other waxes. If you are in a hurry, use base binder spray, and let it dry thoroughly before corking it smooth.

Always apply at least two or three layers of hard wax on top of base binder, to cover it well. It's tough, sticky stuff: in direct contact with snow, it picks up snow particles, which causes icing and slows skis.

Klisters must be applied warm. When cold, you cannot coax a klister out of its tube, not even with brute force. Start by piercing a hole in the ferrule to open the tube; caps have a sharp point for this purpose. If the klister refuses to flow when you squeeze the tube, remember what honey is like when you take it out of the refrigerator: warm the tube slightly, over a radiator or in your hand. Then squeeze the klister out onto the base. Some skiers prefer to squeeze out in longer, straight strips, while others prefer shorter diagonal strips. Smooth out the klister with the plastic spreader paddle packed with the tube. Some skiers like to spread klister and work it into ski bases using the base of their palm. If

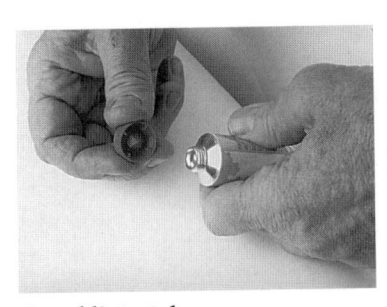

Open klister tube

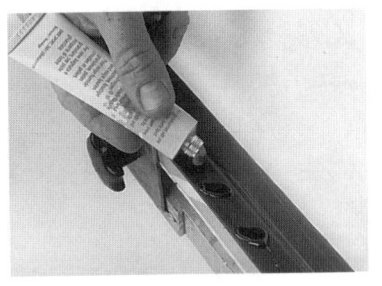

Apply klister in small strips, or one long strip on either side of tracking groove

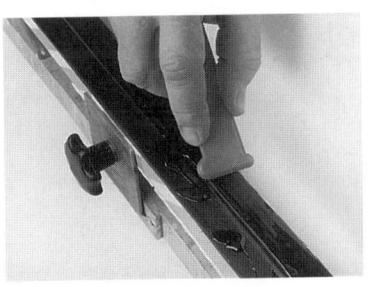

Spread klister with paddle

you don't mind the sticky approach and have hand cleaner handy, hand spreading is an excellent way to get the job done.

There's a one-word rule for applying klisters: *Thin!*. Apply klister about as thick as a coat of paint, no more. As soon as you've finished squeezing klister onto your ski bases, put the cap back on the tube. This simple step spares you the mess that carpers claim is klister's disadvantage. Klister can continue to flow after you have squeezed the tube, not to mention what might happen if you drop the tube on the floor and then step on it. Avoid these problems and you'll become a klister fan. Klisters almost always grip better than hard waxes; if you have the right klister, you're assured secure traction. On the snows for which it is designed, nothing can beat it. Just ask any Australian cross-country skier.

Klister-waxes for the troublesome 1° to 3°C (34° to 37°F) range, come in cans like hard wax, but behave more like klisters. If in doubt, dab a fingertip on top of the wax. If it sticks in tacky strings when you pull your finger off, it's a klister-wax, or a sibling requiring like treatment. Start applying klister-wax like hard wax, by peeling of a strip of the container. But don't crayon it on, as rubbing may cause it to come off onto the base in unmanageable clumps. Instead, dab the wax against the base at intervals about equal to the diameter of the wax can. Rub the dabbed-on wax smooth with a waxing cork; keep a separate cork for this purpose, as the klister wax it picks up can come out and contaminate any harder waxes you cork out. You can also use the base of your palm. The rule for the final layer thickness is the same as for klister: thin!

Beware hand rubbing of klister and klister-wax! The friction created is so great that it can quickly cause a blister. If your hands are not callused by manual work, use a cork and save your skin!

For more grip, both for hard waxes and for klisters, increase the length waxed in the kick zone, preferably slightly more towards the tip than towards the tail, as the tail glide zone is most important in skiing downhill stretches of track.

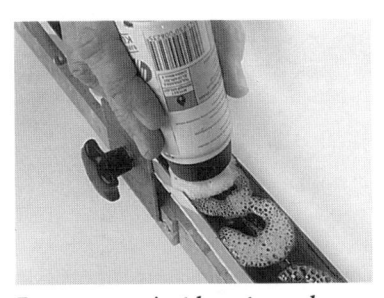
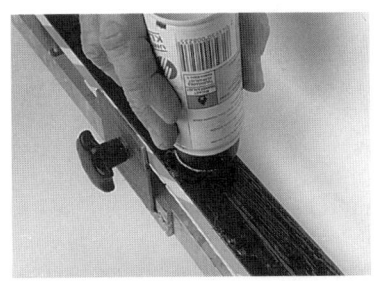

Press can against base to apply spray klister

Smooth spray klister with light touch

Spray klisters are a convenient, speedy alternative to tube klisters, particularly for **Easy waxing** of many pairs of skis (which makes it a favorite for springtime family ski tours). With the can warmed to room temperature, press the top sponge applicator against the base, and dot klister onto it, at intervals about equal to the diameter of the can. Then, with less pressure against the base, use the applicator to spread the klister.

BASES

For the first few thousand years of over-snow travel, skis and sled runners were made of wood. No more. With few exceptions, modern skis and snowboards are made of plastics, fiberglass, metals, and composites. Look at a modern ski or snowboard, and most of what you see is plastic: on top, on the sides, and on the bases. If it's an Alpine ski, you see steel in the edges along the base. Fiberglass, aluminum, or composites gives it strength. Wood, if used at all, is hidden inside, in the core.

Properties of plastics

Plastics is the generic name of a large class of organic, man-made materials that are hard in their finished state, but softer or even liquid at some stage of their manufacture. The body of knowledge of plastics is enormous (for further details see the "bible" of the field, the *International Plastics Handbook* by Hansjürgen Saechtling, 1992, Munich, Carl Hanser Verlag, ISBN 3-446-14924-4, or New York, Oxford University Press, ISBN 0-19-5207637-1). As a skier or snowboarder, you need only know the what and why of the plastics commonly used in bases.

All plastics classify as *polymers* (from the Greek *poly*, many, and *metros*, parts), because they comprise gigantic molecules. There are also many natural polymers, including proteins, cellulose, and starch.

Plastics may be either *thermoplastic*, which can be resoftened and remolded without alteration of basic properties, or *thermosetting*, which cannot be resoftened after initial manufacture. The first plastics included celluloid (1892), a thermoplastic, and bakelite (1909), a thermosetting plastic.

Industrial-scale plastics technologies are relatively new, as the nature of gigantic polymer molecules was long a mystery. In 1920, German chemist Hermann Staudinger (1881-1965) put forth the first theory of them. It was rejected by most of his peers; after one of his lectures, a fellow chemist remarked that "we are as shocked as zoologists might be if they were told that somewhere in Africa, an elephant was found that was 1,500 feet long and 300 feet high." But Staudinger's theories proved correct, which led to understanding of polymers and triggered the growth of the plastics industry. For his discoveries in macro-molecular chemistry, Staudinger was awarded the 1953 Nobel Prize in Chemistry.

All plastics molecules comprise repetitions of a base unit called a *monomer*. Monomers link together in long chains to form polymers. In their natural state and not subjected to external forces, the long monomer chains lie tangled in a jumbled heap, like wet cooked spaghetti on your plate. This disorderly state is called *amorphous*. Forces applied to an amorphous plastic create order, called *crystallization*, in which physical connections are made between molecules. Almost all plastics contain material in the amorphous state and material in the crystalline state. Crys-

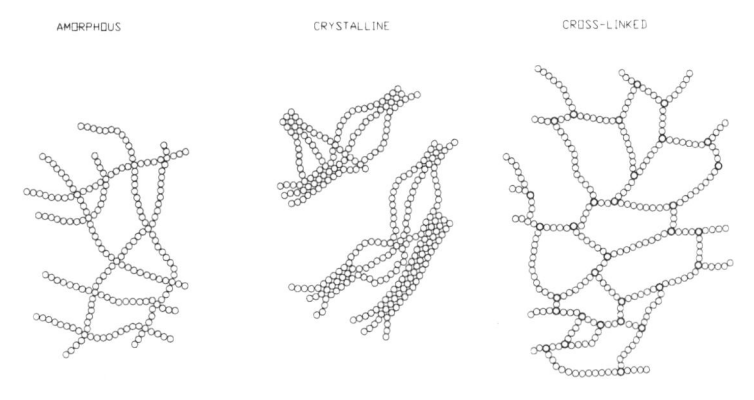

AMORPHOUS   CRYSTALLINE   CROSS-LINKED

Plastics in natural state are amorphous with long molecules in heaps (left); forces cause crystallization (middle); chemical bonding results in cross-linking (right).

tallinity gives a plastic strength and rigidity, while amorphousness gives it elasticity. So the fundamental way of controlling the properties of a plastic is to fix the percentage of crystalline material. Crystallization is a physical process, which can be reversed. So the result of crystallization is a thermoplastic.

Polymer molecules can connect to one another by creating chemical bonds. The resultant three-dimensional network is said to be *cross-linked*. So the properties of a plastic may also be controlled by regulating the degree of cross-linking. Cross-linking is a chemical process, which when complete, cannot be reversed. So its result is a thermosetting plastic.

Manipulating the degrees of crystallization and cross-linking provides innumerable variations of the generic plastic material, called a *binder*. Binders may be made from natural polymers, cellulose, or synthetic resins that have undergone polymerization. *Plasticizers* are added to binders for greater strength and flexibil-

Action of water drop on base indicates glide: better glide if drop stays round; poorer glide if it spreads.

ity. *Fillers* are added for specific characteristics, including impact strength and hardness. *Pigments* add color. *Additives* may result in special properties and often comprise the only differences among tradenamed plastics of the same family. *Antioxidants* are one of the most common types of additives used in the plastics of ski and snow-board bases. Their purpose is to retard oxidation caused by heat and exposure to sunlight. Plastics may also be treated, as with radioactive irradiation, to produce still more varieties of the basic forms.

The properties of a plastic then depend on its ingredients and the manner of their combination. So a plastic may differ from a sibling plastic of its family because its binder molecule is of a different size. The sizes of polymer molecules, like all molecules, are expressed in terms of their molecular weights. The molecular weight of a molecule is the sum of the atomic weights of its constituent atoms, expressed in *amu* (atomic mass units) and can be calculated from its molecular formula. For instance, the most familiar common molecule is water, H_2O. The atomic weight of hydrogen is about 1 amu, and that of oxygen is 16 amu, so the molecular weight of water is $2 \times 1 + 16 = 18$.

The polymer molecules in plastics have not just three, but thousands of atoms of elements heavier than hydrogen and oxygen. Consequently, their molecular weights range from a few hundred thousand amu to a few million amu. A high molecular weight means only that the molecules in a plastic are long; it does not mean that the plastic is heavy. The density (weight relative to that of water) of most plastics used for bases is from 0.9 to 1.05. Most base plastics float in water, or almost so.

Base plastics are made in a wide variety of physical properties and molecular weights. A plastic is termed "high-molecular" or "high-density" if its molecular weight is toward the upper end of the range for its type, and conversely for "low-density" or "low-molecular." In general, high molecular plastics are harder and more durable, but more expensive and less easily handled in production than their low-molecular relatives.

Polyethylene

Polyethylene (PE) is a plastic derived from ethylene gas. It is widely used, such as in packaging, bottles and shower curtains. Arguably it is the most common base plastic on skis and snowboards, and accordingly is available in a wide range of types, compounds, tradenames, and molecular weights. The border between low and high molecular polyethylenes is around 300,000 amu. Most common base polyethylenes are in the lower end of the high-molecular range, with weights up to around 500,000 amu. Up to that weight, the polyethylene sheets used to make bases are manufactured by continuous extrusion, which involves squeezing the plastic out through a die.

Polyethylenes with molecular weights greater than 500,000 amu are called Ultra-High Molecular Weight PE (UHMWPE). Base sheets of UHMWPE cannot be formed by extrusion. They are machined from sintered blocks. Sintering involves subjecting granular plastic to heat and pressure in a press, until the granules weld together to a solid. This process and the subsequent machining to produce base sheets are together complex than extrusion. Consequently, UHMWPE bases are the more expensive. But they are more resistant to wear, hold wax better, and glide better than their low-molecular counterparts.

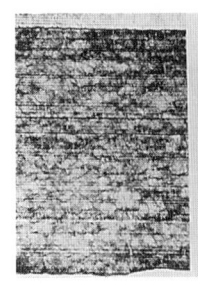

Microscopic view of base cross-section: between particles of sintered base (left) there is more space for wax than in extruded base (right).

Polypropylene

Polypropylene (PP) is derived from propane gas, which, when mixed with butane, is the liquefied petroleum gas (LPG) that powers busses and taxis in many cities. It has a high melting point, 250°F, and is light in weight, and consequently is used both for objects that must be sterilized and for nautical ropes and floats. Polypropylene bases are available in a wide range of molecular weights. Compared to polyethylene on a base, polypropylene is "slower" because it glides less well, particularly on cold, dry snow. But it is dryer and slightly easier to wax. And it's cheaper.

ABS

ABS (acrylonitrile butadiene styrene) is derived from butane (acrylic rubber) and styrene and is available in a range of molecular weights. It is a good electrical insulator, molds easily, and has high impact strength. So its common uses include telephone and electronic equipment housings, refrigerator parts, pleasure-boat hulls, and car-body parts. ABS ski and snowboard bases glide well on almost all snows, but are not as fast as polyethylene bases. ABS bases hold wax well and are easy to wax when cold. They are hard and durable and resist abrasion well, but tolerate heat poorly, making them difficult to hot wax or hot wax clean. Consequently, when used in bases, ABS usually is compounded with other materials to produce a plastic superior to basic ABS.

Flaws in bases

Bases can be defective when new and can be damaged in use. The most common defects and damage are:

Base burn: a whitened, roughened, apparently dry area, most visible on a dark-colored base, usually caused by use on abrasive, artificial snow.

Cuts and scratches caused by sharp objects, including parts of ski racks, rocks and gravel in snow, and tools used inadvertently.

Lack of flatness: Bases may lack crosswise flatness by being *railed* (concave) or *bowed* (convex).

See **Care and Repair** for ways to correct these flaws.

BASE PREPARATION

Base preparation is like a car engine tune-up. It should always be done when a pair of skis or a snowboard is new. How often and how thoroughly it is repeated thereafter depends on the snow conditions where you ski or snowboard and the performance you seek. Occasional base preparation never hurts, even if you are an infrequent, recreational skier or snowboarder. Like a periodic car engine tune-up, it ensures continued on-snow usefulness. More frequent base preparation is for racers and others who seek performance. As in car racing, part of preparation is done before every race. Waxes are now so accurately matched to snows that in any one race, chances are that most of the racers have seen the same weather and the same snow data, and accordingly have used the same wax. So any advantage of better performance that one racer may have over another comes not from the final waxing, but from base preparation. That's why racers and their technicians spend so much time at it.

A good guide for recreational skiers and snowboarders is to prepare bases when new and then again whenever their gliding surfaces seem dry or no longer feel soapy to the touch. Base preparation and glide waxing (see **Applying wax**) are similar processes and use similar - and sometimes the same - glide waxes. The basic difference is that in base preparation you work more to mechanically alter the base and to better bond the glide wax to it.

Always start preparation with dry, clean bases (see **Cleaning bases**), in good repair (see **Care and repair**).

Alpine skis, Telemark skis, jumping skis, and snowboards

New skis: The factory finish on most new bases is acceptable. If not, you may wish to smooth it by **Stone grinding** or wet-belt sanding at a suitably equipped shop, or by scraping with a sharp ski scraper and sanding with #100 sandpaper, followed by buffing with a nylon pad. Check steel edges and file them if necessary (see **Edge filing**). With the ski or board firmly fixed, base up, iron in a base-preparation glide wax. Scrape the wax when it is still partly molten. Repeat the process at least three times. Then let the wax cool, about 15 to 20 minutes at room temperature. Finally, scrape off excess wax, and finish with a nylon-bristle brush. See **Applying wax** for the techniques involved. Rill the

Scrape new base with steel scraper

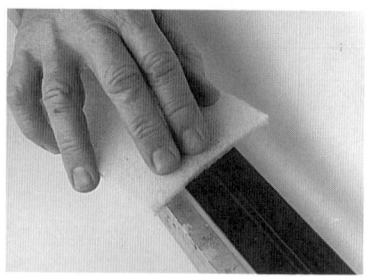
Buff with nylon pad

Melt wax onto base with warm iron

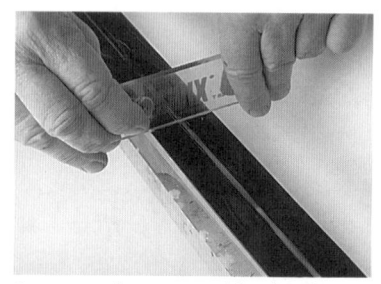
Scrape molten wax with plastic scraper

Scrape off excess cooled wax with a plastic scraper

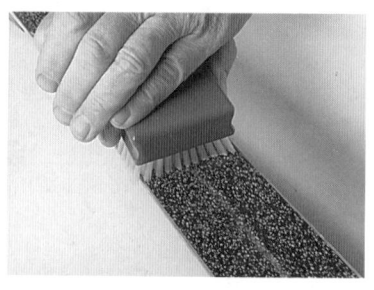
Then brush base smooth

bases (see **Rilling**) if you wish to improve stability or turning ability. New bases are usually rilled by **Stone grinding**.

Race day: Scrape off any protective wax previously put on before transportation or storage, and brush the base smooth. Then check for scratches and edge damage, and repair if need be (see **Care and repair** and **Edge filing**). Then, if you seek greater stability or turning ability, rill the base (see **Rilling**). Use a steel or stiff brass bristle brush or #100 sandpaper. Draw the brush or sandpaper longitudinally and in a straight line, from tip towards

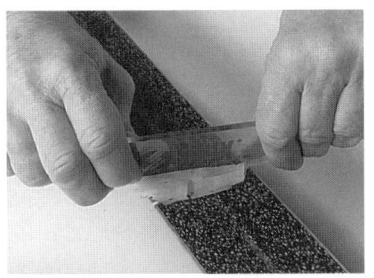

On race day, first scrape off protective wax with a plastic scraper

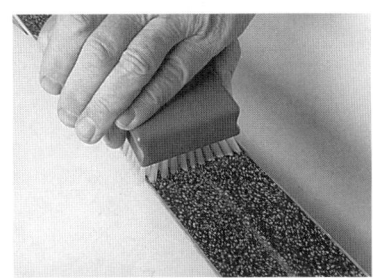

Then brush base smooth

tail. Use a sharp steel scraper to remove any excess material raised and loosened by rilling. Repeat preparation waxing after rilling a base. Then you are ready to select and apply the wax of the day (see **Mixing charts** and **Applying wax**).

Rill with sandpaper in a block, if needed

Cross-country skis

New skis: The factory finish on new recreational skis usually is acceptable. But most new performance-ski bases need some touching up. With a ski firmly fixed, base up, lightly sand the entire base and lightly round its edges with #100 sandpaper. Use a steel scraper or nylon scouring pad to remove any burrs.

Then, if you wish, rill the base (see **Rilling**). Follow the manufacturer's directions in using a riller. First, select the rilling iron for the snow on which you intend to ski. Push the rilling tool along the base, from tip towards tail. Use firm pressure and long, even strokes. After sanding or rilling, use a steel scraper to remove burrs and sharp edges and then buff smooth with wiping tissue.

Locate the **kick zone** of classical cross-country skis, and sand it with #100 sandpaper.

Finally, iron in a base-preparation glide wax, on the glide zones of a classical ski or over the entire base of a skating ski. Scrape the wax when it is still partly molten. Repeat the process at least three times. Then let the wax cool, about 15 to 20 minutes at room temperature. Finally, scrape off excess wax, and fin-

Sand new cross-country ski base flat with sandpaper wrapped around a scraper

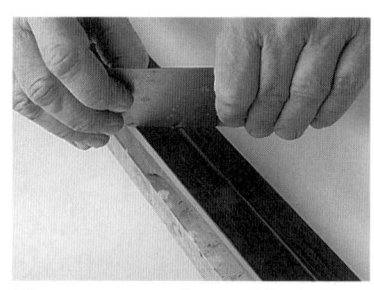

Then scrape new base with steel scraper

Rill base with even strokes of a rilling iron

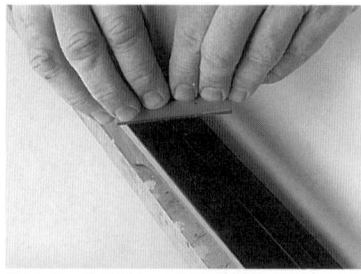

Level off rill peaks with razor blade scraper

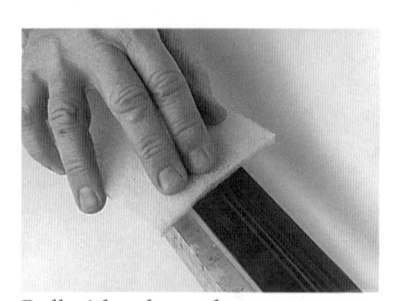

Buff with nylon pad

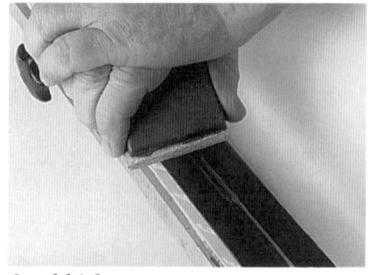

Sand kick zone

ish with a nylon-bristle brush. See **Applying wax** for the techniques involved.

Race Day: Scrape off any protective wax previously put on before transportation or storage, and brush the base smooth. Then check for scratches and repair if need be (see **Care and repair**). Re-rill the bases if necessary to suit the day's conditions. Repeat preparation waxing after rilling a base. Then you are ready to select and apply the wax of the day (see **Mixing charts** and **Applying wax**).

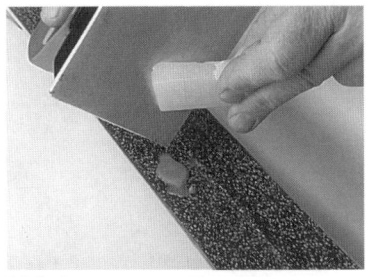

Melt base preparation glide wax onto base with warm iron

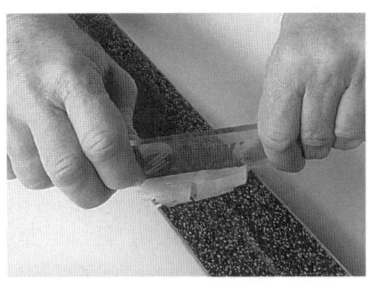

Scrape off excess cooled wax with a plastic scraper

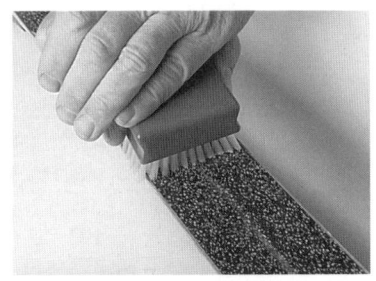

Finish with nylon brushing

On race day, first scrape off excess wax with a plastic scraper

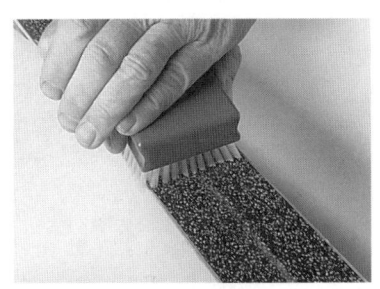

Then brush base smooth

Smooth edges with sandpaper

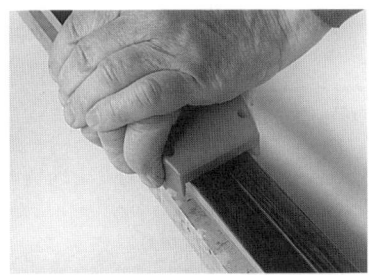

Rill base with even strokes of a rilling iron, if needed

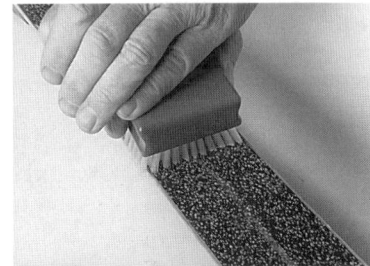

Brush along base

CARE AND REPAIR

Clean your skis or snowboard, preferably after use and always before storing or transporting for a few days or more. Wax and dirt on plastics harden with time and are then more difficult to remove. See **Cleaning Bases** for details.

Repair base burn (abrasion of bases by artificial snow) whenever you wax. First, scrape the affected area to remove the fuzz that gives the burn its whitish appearance, using a sharp steel scraper. Then lightly sand the area, using #200 sandpaper. Finally, prepare the affected area or the whole base anew; see **Base preparation**.

Repair other base damage as soon as possible. First, be sure that the base material can be repaired. Almost all polyethylene bases can be repaired using hand tools. Some ABS bases may require professional shop repair. If in doubt, consult the instructions or guarantee or ask the shop that sold the skis or board.

For polyethylene base repair, start by cleaning the affected area. Use wax remover solvent and wiping tissue to remove all foreign matter from a cut or scrape. Trim loose edges. Then, fill the cavity with molten polyethylene. There are two methods, depending on the repair material (sold by ski/snowboard shops) and tools you have on hand.

Use iron to melt polyethylene strip and fill cavity

1) "Iron a strip:" clip a short length of rectangular polyethylene strip, and hold it on the base, over the cavity. Use a waxing iron, set on medium to high, to melt the strip down, even with the base or slightly above it.

2) "Candle:" if you don't have an iron on hand for repairs, use a polyethylene base-repair stick as a "candle." Light the end of it and drip molten polyethylene down on the horizontal base, to fill slightly over the surrounding level of the base.

Let the fill cool for 30 minutes or more. Then use a steel scraper to remove the excess and flatten the fill even with the base. Finally, smooth the fill with #200 or finer sandpaper.

Also repair cuts and scratches in tops and sides as soon as possible, and at least once a year, in the spring before storage for the summer. Repairs to sides are more urgent than repairs to tops. Deep cuts in sides can let water seep into the internal core, which will weaken it. Top sheets usually are thick, so damage to them is mostly cosmetic. Start repair by cleaning the damaged area. Then fill it with two-component epoxy filler (available at ski/ snowboard shops, but some automotive-body-repair fillers work well). Let the epoxy harden for a day or so, and then scrape the fill flush with the surrounding surface.

Check base flatness after all repairs or whenever on-snow performance, such as tracking (the ability to run straight), seems to change. Place a steel base scraper, or any tool with a good

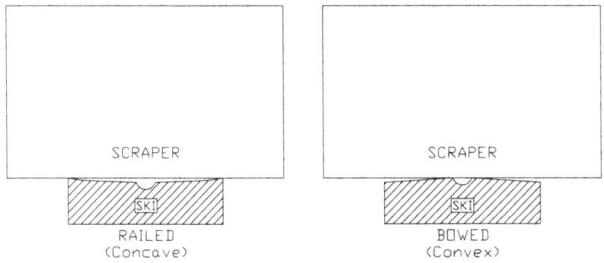

Sight under straightedge to check for railed (left) or bowed (right) base

straightedge, on the base. Sight lengthwise along the base, with a light behind the straightedge. If you see an opening at the center, the base is railed. If you see openings at the edges, or if you can rock the straightedge from edge to edge, the base is bowed.

Slight crosswise curvature, up to a few hundredths of an inch, has little effect on performance. Greater curvature can affect performance, particularly for narrower cross-country skis, for which base flatness dictates tracking. Flatten a railed or bowed base by drawing a steel scraper along it, with the ski firmly fixed horizontally, base up. Curvature of Alpine ski bases is more difficult to correct, as steel edges interfere with scraping. Flattening Alpine ski bases is a shop job; see **Stone Grinding**. Unless serious, curvature of broader jumping skis, which run in tracks on the inrun and on flat-packed snow on the outrun, seldom needs correction. Flattening jumping ski bases is also a job for ski-shop stone grinding. For broad snowboard bases, ripples are more of a problem than curvature across the entire base. Sight across the base using a long straightedge. Mark any ripples you see with a felt marking pen, and then sand them flat with #200 sandpaper.

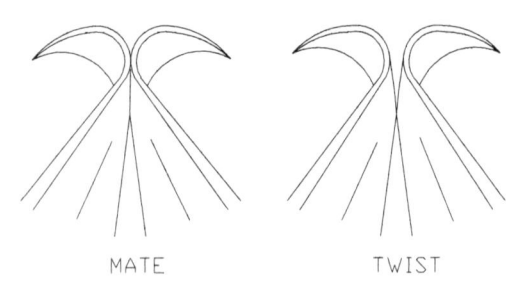

MATE   TWIST

Sight along pair held base-to-base to check for twist

Check ski pair straightness, closure, and mate. With two hands, hold a pair of skis, with the footplate just behind the binding in each palm. First, check straightness by holding the pair vertically, base against base, tails on the floor. The bases should touch each other over their full widths, at two places, behind the tips and in front of the tails. Check for that correct mate by holding one ski still.

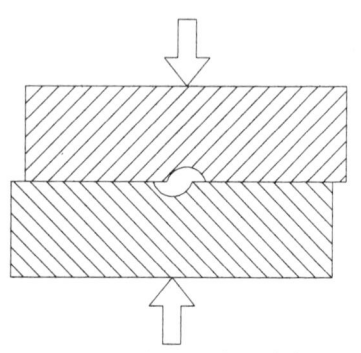

With tips and tails aligned, base-to-base midsection mismatch indicates warp

Rotate your other hand slightly, as if turning the cap of a jar, to try to rock the other ski back and forth against the ski held still. If you cannot rock the ski, the pair is straight. But if you can rock one ski back and forth against the other, or hear a slight click-click as the bases touch when you rock, one or possibly both skis may be warped. Warp can be serious, as it will cause a ski to yaw, or always turn in one direction of its own accord. So if you suspect warp, first exactly align the skis with each other, where they touch near their tips and tails, and then squeeze the mid points together. The midpoints, or waists, of the skis should meet exactly. If they do not, one or both skis may be warped in the crosswise direction. Then pick up the pair and sight along the bases from tail to tip, when the tails are held together. You should see the bases touch together over their entire width, where they meet just behind the ski tip. If you see a vee-shaped gap, one or both skis are twisted by warp. Even if the skis meet as they should, both may be warped. Check for this defect by reversing one ski, holding the pair with one tail against the other tip, and resighting. Correcting warp is a job for a well-equipped ski-repair shop. As warp is sometimes due to a factory defect, you should check for it before buying a new pair of skis.

Check closure by sighting between the bases as you squeeze the pair together at the midpoint. The bases should close evenly and smoothly, with no high or low points and no gaps in between points where the bases touch. Mark and then remove any bumps, as bumpy bases wear wax unevenly and glide slowly. Check mate by holding the ski bases tightly against each other. They should match along their entire contact length. Slight mismatch, up to 1/32 inch or so, has little effect. But greater mismatch may indicate warp.

Repair delamination, which is the separation of the layers of material that make up a ski or snowboard from each other. Delamination occurs most frequently at one end. First, spread the laminations from each other and block them apart with matchsticks. Clean all surfaces thoroughly with wax remover solvent, and let the solvent evaporate completely. Spread epoxy glue over the more accessible of each facing pair of the surfaces to be joined, remove the matchstick props, and close the laminations together. Apply pressure until the glue cures. C-clamps and blocks are best. If you don't have these tools, wrap the area with strong masking tape, starting farthest from the end, and squeezing the laminations together as you go. When the glue has cured, slit the tape along one edge with a knife, and remove it in one big unwrap. Then trim off any surplus glue that oozed out.

Check binding screws several times a season, and tighten any loose screws. Several types of screws are used to mount bindings, so be sure to use the right type of screwdriver. Pozi-Drive #3 head screws are among the most common, and Pozi-Drive screwdrivers are available at sports shops and hardware stores. In a pinch, you can use the more widely available Phillips screwdriver. But use it sparingly, as its flutes don't match and accordingly can damage Pozi-Drive head screws. Whenever screws turn but don't tighten down, take them out and plug the holes with plastic plugs (available at ski/snowboard shops). Then re-drive the screws.

Check steel edges several times a season or, if you are a racer, each time you wax. See **Edge filing** for sharpening techniques. Otherwise, check for loose edges; edge repair is a job for a well-equipped ski-repair shop. You may use steel wool to remove rust, but preventing rust is always the better strategy. After skiing, wipe edges dry with a small terry-cloth towel, and wax edges before storing at the end of a season; see **Transporting and storing skis.** Always regard rust as a warning sign, particularly if it appears after you have driven with unprotected skis on a roof rack. The clouds of slush particles that are spewed up by traffic on winter roads are often saturated with road salt, which causes steel edges to rust almost instantly. Worse yet, road salt degrades ski bases and attacks bindings, particularly those with aluminum parts. So whenever you see a salt-rusted edge, check the ski's base and binding.

CHOOSING WAXES

Be snow wise

Judging snow is the first and most important step in all waxing. Judge snow right, and waxing is easy; knowledge of snow, not waxes, is what separates the good waxers from those who struggle at it. In order of importance, the factors affecting snow are temperature, structure, and water content. These three factors are related, as shown in the chart below.

When the snow-level air temperature is	Then snow characteristics are determined by
Above freezing	Structure of snow Free water content [snow temperature is constant at 0°C (32°F)]
Below freezing	Structure of snow Snow temperature [free water content is constant at nearly zero]

The two categories, above and below freezing, jibe with everyday experience and with the lingo of weather forecasts. If the snow-level air temperature is well below freezing, -4°C (25°F) or below, almost all the liquid, or "free," water in the snow is frozen; the snow is said to be *dry*. If the snow-level air temperature is well above freezing, +1°C (34°F) or above, the snow usually contains liquid water, which because it can then run, is said to be "free;" the snow is said to be *wet*.

Temperature

The temperature ranges stated on wax containers are air temperatures at snow level. But the temperature shown on an outdoor thermometer may differ from snow-level temperature, especially when a thermometer is mounted high above the snow or exposed to the sun or another heat source, such as the window of a heated building. Also, new snow may be colder or warmer than the air temperature just above the snow surface. There are two ways around this dilemma.

First, you may regard temperature as a rough guide only, and check the snow. One of the best checks is to grab a handful of snow in a gloved hand, squeeze it hard, and then open your hand. If the snow is loose and powdery or blows away when you open your hand, it's dry. If it forms a snowball or large clumps, it's wet (see **Snow types**).

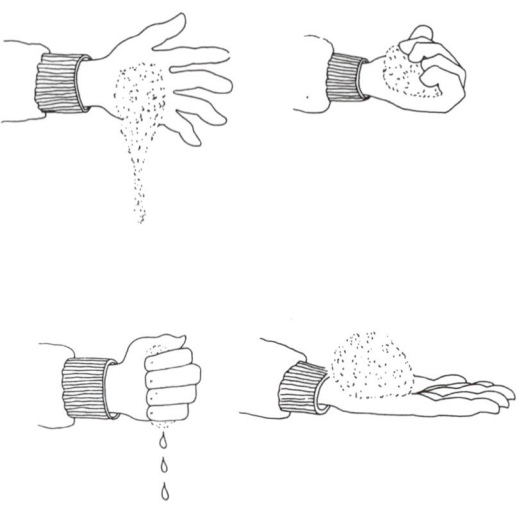

With hand in glove or mitten, squeeze a handful of snow; dry snow will blow away when you open your hand; wet snow forms a snowball; very wet snow drips.

Second, if you race or otherwise seek accurate waxing, you may measure temperature yourself. Do this by holding the bulb or detector of a suitable thermometer (see **Tools** for more on waxing thermometers) just at the snow surface. If the snow is exposed to direct sunlight, shield the thermometer so it is in shadow for a few minutes, as it might otherwise be heated by the sunlight and consequently misread.

Snow structure

Snow structure depends on the nature of the snow when it fell and on the weather that has influenced it since it fell. For most waxing purposes, snow is usually classified according to its content of free water as *dry* or *wet* and according to its stage in the process of continual change in a snow cover as *new* (falling or newly fallen snow), *fine-grained* (older snow, with crystals rounded), and *coarse-grained* (snow that has frozen so individual grains form larger grains). Wax manufacturers often add to these basic terms, regrettably in an inconsistent manner. Fortunately, most manufacturers now adhere to standard snow terminology; see **Snow types** for further details.

Water

At temperatures several degrees removed from freezing, snow is either completely wet or completely dry, and judging it for waxing is relatively easy. However, at temperatures close to freezing, judging snow is ticklish, because snow properties change rapidly with small changes of temperature and free-water content. That's when a waxing thermometer's indication of snow-surface temperature is the sensible first resort.

Humidity

The directions on almost all wax containers assume an average winter relative air humidity of 60% to 80%. But wintertime humidity does vary from the average, particularly in North America, where both Canada and the USA have large areas of continental climates. New snow at -5°C (23°F) in the coastal Cascades or the Sierra seems wetter or "warmer" than indicated in waxing directions, because the humidity is higher. Likewise, new snow at that same temperature in the inland Rockies seems dryer or "colder" because the humidity is lower. You can compensate for these deviations in two ways. First, you can "wax wetter" in high-humidity regions, and "wax dryer" in dryer regions. Second, you can mix your own waxes; see **Mixing charts**.

Other factors to consider

Exposure: Everyone who lives in the snow belt in the Northern Hemisphere knows that the sun melts snow faster on southern than on northern exposures. (The reverse is true in the Southern Hemisphere). The effect on waxing is obvious: snow in the sun is wetter than snow in the shade. But there's also a hidden effect on snows that get little or no sun. On a clear day, they can lose heat rapidly. This means that although morning air temperatures can rise as surrounding air masses are heated by the sun, snow temperature can remain consistently colder in the shade, which calls for "waxing colder."

Clouds and fog If you ski high, in the clouds or in a fog, you are surrounded by air at nearly 100% humidity, which may soak a snow surface. So you should "wax warmer" than usual. Cloud cover counts, even when you are not on snow. Clouds shield the

Earth from the heat of the sun. But clouds also slow the escape of heat from the Earth to space, which is why clear nights usually are colder than cloudy nights. The reverse effect of cloud cover or lack of it affects waxing in two ways. First, after a clear night, snow temperature can be lower than air temperature for several hours, particularly in midwinter, when the sun is low in the sky. So after a clear night, "wax colder." Second, on a sunny day, sudden overcasts don't lower snow temperature; they raise it because the clouds prevent heat escape from the snow. Anyone who has skied in high mountain areas, such as the Rockies or the Alps, knows the result of this phenomenon: at the top, in the sun, you may wear a down parka, yet feel cold as you start your run. Then you ski into a cloud, and within minutes, you are sweating. Your skis or snowboard act the same way: glide slows on the warmer snow.

Wind can alter a snow surface because it exerts a force that packs the snow particles tightly together. The denser snow acts as if it were older, and glide on it is poorer. **Stone grinding** or **rilling** can improve glide on wind-packed snow.

Albedo (the Latin word for whiteness, a term borrowed from astronomy) is the ratio of the light energy reflected by a snow surface to that falling upon it. The albedo of a snow surface determines how much energy it will absorb from the sun. Typical albedos are:

Snow type	Albedo
Compact, dry, pure snow	86% - 95%
Pure, wet, fine-grained snow	63% - 75%
Pure, wet, corn snow	60% - 62%
Spongy, wet, light gray snow	45% - 47%
Sopping wet, gray snow	40% - 43%
Slushy, dirty snow	about 30%

The wide range of snow albedos explains why a much-skied slope in the sun can be "slower" than a lesser skied but equally exposed slope. Skiing soils snow, which makes it absorb more energy from the sun, which makes it wetter, which, in turn, makes it absorb even more energy from the sun, sometimes two or three times as much as an equivalent unskied slope.

Altitude affects snow character indirectly, as elevation itself has little influence on snow. The greatest difference is that on a still day, temperature usually falls about 3°F for each 1000 foot increase in altitude.

Snow source: All snow crystals are formed by condensation around microscopic particles, called condensation nuclei. Over inland areas, a condensation nucleus most likely will be a dust particle, while over an ocean, it most likely will be a small salt crystal, carried aloft by water evaporated from the sea. So snows which fall on coastal areas often contain microscopic quantities of salt. Normally, salt in snow has little effect on it during a normal winter. However, toward spring, when the customarily heavy coastal snowfalls melt, the salt content of the remaining snow surface may increase appreciably. In turn, this depresses the freezing point of the water on the snow surface, which, for waxing, makes the snow seem wetter than it otherwise might be at the same temperature. Consequently, on coastal snows, you may have to "wax wetter" towards spring.

External influences: Snow in the atmosphere is affected by pollution, as is snow on the ground. Snow in ski areas is affected by packing and grooming. Artificial snow differs from natural snow. Other factors, including inconsistent directions on the container, also affect wax selection. See **Factors other than meteorological** for details.

CLEANING BASES

Always clean bases before applying new wax, repairing or preparing bases or storing a pair of skis or a snowboard. Most waxes on bases will harden within a few days, so if you are a weekend skier or snowboarder, it's best to clean on Sunday or Monday evening, so you won't have a worse mess by Friday. And be sure to clean if you have driven with skis or a snowboard exposed on

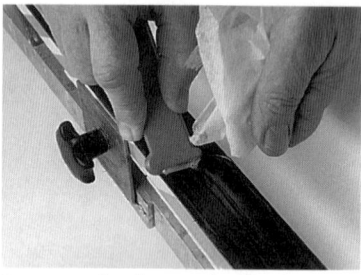

Scrape and wipe; a plastic scraper is best

a car roof rack, as road films, dust and road salt attack and destroy base plastics.

Cleaning is best done indoors; it's usually more comfortable there and waxes are more pliable. Start by using a plastic or metal scraper to remove as much old wax as possible. Some skiers find broad-bladed putty knives handy for the job. But be careful when using a metal blade, as its edges and corners can dig into and damage a plastic base. After you have scraped off as much old wax as possible, remove the rest by heating and wiping, hot scraping, or dissolving and wiping, or a combination of these three basic methods. Always clean sides as well as a base, as old wax on sides collects snow and slows glide.

Heating and wiping is the time-honored way to finish cleaning, hailing from the days when skis, as well as their bases, were made of wood. But it now also is precarious, as heat can oxidize and otherwise damage a base plastic. This is because compared to plastics, wood resists flame well. For most woods, the ignition temperature (at which wood bursts into flame if heated long enough) varies from 220° to 280°C (428° to 536°F), depending on moisture content and the duration of exposure to heat. Wood can also tolerate heat well above its ignition temperature, if the heating is brief. This is why you can use a blowtorch to strip paint off furniture, doors and the like, but not set fire to the underlying wood. Not so with the plastics used on ski and snowboard bases, which when heated, begin to oxidize, soften and melt almost immediately, at temperatures around 150°C (300°F). So always start with caution, first by heating the base with a waxing iron, and then by quickly wiping off the molten wax with wiping tissue or a lint-free rag. Never use a waxing torch for this task, unless you are experienced with it and can keep the flame moving fast enough to just melt the wax, but not singe the base. Dispose of the wax-soaked tissue or rag in a safe place, preferably in a fireproof refuse container.

Hot scraping resembles heating and wiping, with an extra step. Though time consuming, it is the method of choice for racers and professionals, as it is both efficient and easy on base plastics. With a base horizontal, facing up, start by applying and warming a soft glide wax into the entire base, until it is thoroughly warm. Then scrape and wipe off the wax while it is still molten. Repeat the process two or three times to completely remove old wax and contaminants. Finish by letting the skis or snowboard cool for 15 to 20 minutes, to room temperature. Then use a plastic scraper to remove any excess wax, and follow scraping by buffing lightly with lint-free waxing tissue.

Dissolving and wiping with a solvent and a lint-free rag or wiping tissue is the quickest way to finish cleaning. Always follow directions when using solvents, and always use them in well-ventilated places; see **Safety** for a discussion of the hazards involved. The biodegradable, citrus-oil solvents offered by wax manufacturers are best for the task. Never use lighter fluid, gasoline, or turpentine to clean bases. These fluids are not only highly flammable, but they can also dissolve base plastics or, at best, leave a surface film that repels wax. Always dispose of rags and tissue used in a safe place, preferably in a fireproof refuse container.

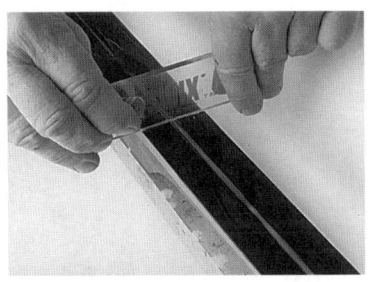 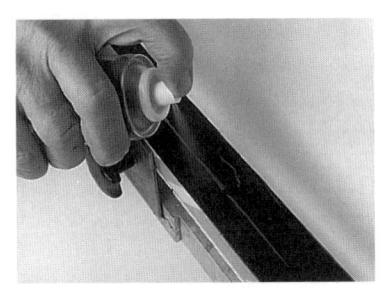

Scrape molten wax with a plastic scraper   *Pump spray solvents ease cleaning*

CONSTITUENT MATERIALS

Ski and snowboard waxes are compounded from many ingredients, each with a particular mission in determining the final characteristics of a wax.

Glide waxes for all skiing and snowboarding

Petroleum waxes: Paraffin waxes (macrocrystalline) waxes comprise the backbone of most second-generation waxes. The softer paraffins are preferable in waxes blended to match wet snow. Microcrystalline waxes are used to improve flexibility, as most normal paraffins are hard and brittle.

Synthetic paraffin waxes are used in waxes for colder snows.

Mineral waxes are used to modify paraffin waxes.

Fluorocarbons are used in third-generation waxes, such as in pure fluorocarbon powders, or as additives to hydrocarbon waxes.

Solid lubricants, such as graphite and metal particles, are used to attain special characteristics. Graphite, which is a slippery material, is used in waxes to improve glide at low air humidities and on icy snows.

Additives are usually of *hydrophobic* (water-repelling) materials, used in small dosages to improve glide on some snows.

Grip or "Kick" waxes for cross-country

Hard waxes and klisters contain the same spectrum of ingredients, as both must grip on snow. The selection of ingredients and their proportions determine hardness.

Petroleum waxes: Microcrystalline waxes are most used.

High-molecular synthetic rubber is the constituent that sets grip waxes apart from glide waxes. It provides flexibility, internal cohesion and adhesion to ski bases, so snow can penetrate the wax at the instant of a kick, yet not wear too fast on the base.

White oil and petroleum jelly are used to soften synthetic resins and esters, which otherwise are hard when cold; oil content is higher in waxes for wet snows than in waxes for cold snows.

Synthetic resins are the main ingredient in klisters and in some klister-waxes.

Fluorocarbons are added in small quantities to improve glide without sacrificing grip.

Solid lubricants are used to improve glide and attain the right wax consistency.

Additives are used in smaller quantities, to achieve particular characteristics and to facilitate the production process.

EASY WAXING

Adventure skier Ned Gillette once remarked that "waxing may be a little more complicated than making a peanut-butter-and-jelly sandwich, but the aim is to keep it simple." Gillette spoke of cross-country skiing (in his 1979 book by that title), but his message applies to all of skiing and snowboarding: the simple, easy approach is often best for the situation at hand.

Glide waxing for Alpine skis, Telemark skis, snowboards, and cross-country skating skis

What you need
- One of the forms of glide wax: block, paste, aerosol or pump spray, or fluid. See **Glide waxes** for descriptions.
- Solvent, preferably biodegradable citrus oil, for cleaning bases.
- Waxing cork.
- Wiping tissue.

How to do it

Start with a clean base. If it is dirty, soak it with solvent and wipe clean with a rag, then dry with wiping tissue. Let the base dry thoroughly, then apply the glide wax. Spread it out to a thin layer, with either a waxing cork or wiping tissue. Finally, polish smooth with a waxing cork.

Hold ski upright and crayon wax on entire base

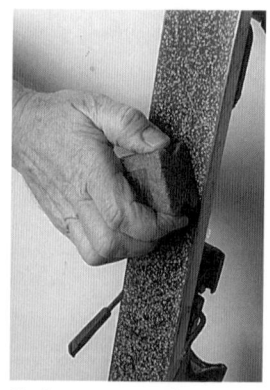

Cork wax smooth

Grip waxing for classical cross-country skis

What you need

- Two-wax pack, with a blue wax for cold snow and a red wax for new, moist, or wet snow.
- Universal klister spray for changed snow or old, wet snow.
- Universal glider for cross-country.
- Solvent, preferably biodegradable citrus oil, for cleaning bases.
- Waxing cork.
- Wiping tissue.

How to do it

Start with a clean base. If it is dirty, soak it with solvent and wipe clean with a rag, then dry with wiping tissue. Let the base dry thoroughly. Then wax, first for glide, then for grip. Start by crayoning glide wax onto the tip and tail glide zones, and then corking it smooth. When you are finished, select the grip wax of the day: dry or wet hard wax or universal klister. Apply a hard wax as you did the glide wax, by crayoning it on the kick zone, and then corking it smooth. If it's a klister day, spray or dab and spread the klister, depending on whether it is in an aerosol spray can or a dab applicator can. Finally, smooth the klister with a light touch.

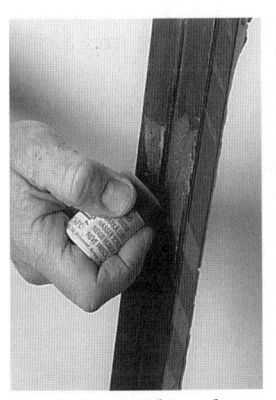  

Hold ski upright and crayon grip wax on kick zone

Cork hard wax smooth

Hold ski upright and press can against base to apply spray klister

EDGE FILING

Steel edges on Alpine skis and snowboards both enable accurate control and protect bases. Almost all edges are now *hidden*, with part of the edge recessed under the base plastic sheet. Although this construction boosts performance, it complicates edge repair, as the fastenings or bond between an edge and the interior core are underneath the base. In turn, this places a premium on edge maintenance to ensure consistent performance.

Most recreational skiers and snowboarders want products that require as little care as possible. Accordingly, the edges on recreational skis and boards are made of harder steel than those on their racing siblings, as the harder the steel, the longer the edge holds its sharpness. The drawback is that harder edges are more difficult to file. Racers, who need extremely sharp edges and usually file before each race, need the ease of filing afforded by softer edge steel.

Bevels ease control

The theoretical right-angled edge is flush with the ski base and flush with the sidewall at an angle of 90° to the base. Some edges are made this way, but most are *beveled,* or angled away from the flat, in one or two ways. Beveled edges both lower edge pressure on snow when riding a flat ski or board and ease turn initiation. A *bevel* is a slight angle, usually 0.5° to 1°, below the surface of the base (or "above" it, if you think of the base in its position on snow). A *side bevel* is a corresponding angle, usually about 2° but sometimes as much as 4°, more inwards. These angles are typical; for exact angles, see the manufacturer's recommendations for your skis or snowboard, as bevel angles are only a part of the overall design for control on snow.

Be guided in filing

Though skilled technicians can hand-file edges using only a file, most skiers and snowboarders - and an increasing number of technicians - now use a file guide, which is a holder with an adjustment that fixes the file firmly at a selected bevel angle. Most file guides come in sets, with one or more file blades specifically designed for edge steels. File guide configurations and blade surfaces vary considerably, so there is no one procedure that

File base face of edge

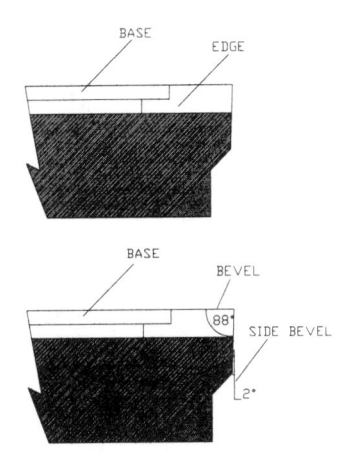

Bevel and side bevel are slight angles

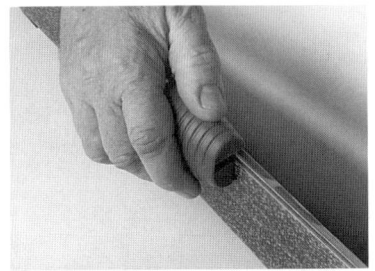

Use holder to file side face of edge

applies to all filing. But common to all is *draw filing,* which is pulling or pushing the file in its guide along the edge in an action similar to that of using a carpenter's plane.

Edges may also be dressed by machine; see **Stone grinding**. These machines work by pressing a ski down against grinding wheels. The pressure compresses the base plastic slightly. It rebounds after coming out of the machine. The result is that the steel edges may then be slightly below the surface of the base, by a hundredth of an inch or so.

Polishing

Even a slight burr can degrade edge performance and consequently complicate control. Pits, as caused by rust, can collect ice and destroy edge action. So it's wise to always polish edges after filing, as well as before storing skis or a snowboard. Use a polishing stone, preferably in a holder, as available from wax manufacturers, and run it flat over the entire edge. Polishing edges improves control in turns.

Combating case hardening

When a steel edge hits a rock at speed, the friction and impact cause a surge of local heating, which tempers the surface of the edge, making it harder than the surrounding metal. In metallurgy, the process is intentional and is known as *case hardening*. Unintentional case hardening, of smaller areas along an edge, will cause a file to bite unevenly (and may even dull it) as it is drawn along an edge. So, if you see the telltale burnished blue of a case-hardened area, remove it with a whetstone before filing. Again, a guide for the stone eases the task and helps retain edge profile.

Detuning

Sharp edges, where they are not needed, can be dangerous. So it's wise to *detune*, or round off, the lengths of edges not in contact with snow at tip and tail. Use a file or flexible abrasive stone made for the purpose.

FACTORS OTHER THAN METEOROLOGICAL

Factors other than meteorological conditions can alter snow on the ground and influence the choices made in waxing. As global warming makes winter weather less and less predictable and races are held on ever tighter schedules, ski areas and race organizers have increasingly resorted to artificial snow, which, because it is made on site, differs from natural, atmospheric snow. Airborne pollutants, sometimes carried with new snow but most frequently deposited on site, contaminate snow and change its properties. Snow on the ground is also deliberately altered, usually to suit it for racing.

Artificial snow

Whenever you see TV coverage of a meet at which no snow is visible in the background, you know that it's on artificial snow. The same holds for the ski area that you travel to through a snowless countryside, to find snow when there otherwise is none. Though a godsend for meet organizers and ski-area operators, artificial snow is not the same as the natural stuff. This is because it usually is made from local groundwater or surface water. Groundwater is sometimes too warm to be used for making snow. Whenever the air temperature is around freezing or just below, the snow-making machinery cannot cope with water that is several degrees warmer. Consequently, groundwater is sometimes pumped into tanks above ground and allowed to cool before being used, which is yet another way in which the water can differ from that in the atmosphere. In the snow-making machinery, the water is pumped to pressure and sprayed out through a nozzle to form a mist of droplets, which then freeze to become ice particles. The resultant artificial snow is harder and denser than natural atmospheric snow at the same air temperature. So on new artificial snow, you must wax about 4°C (7°F) "colder" than on natural snow at the same temperature. On older, settled artificial snow, the difference is less. On corn snow, which results from repeated freeze-thaw cycles, there is little difference between snows of natural and snows of artificial origin.

Polluted snow

Airborne pollutants can be carried with snowstorms, sometimes over considerable distances. In Norway, where this book was written, snowfalls are often grayed by industrial pollutants spewed into the atmosphere by smokestack industries in Great Britain. Though of concern to farmers, foresters and ecologists, who fear the effects of acid rain (and snow), atmospheric pollutants carried in snow usually have little effect on waxing. Worse are the pollutants deposited on snow from nearby sources. Studies made in Switzerland have shown that a heavily-trafficked highway in the floor of a valley can have far-reaching effects on the snows on the slopes above. Smog created by motor-vehicle emissions can warm snows, which, of course, makes them wetter. In worst cases, Alpine valley smogs have increased the frequency of avalanches, as pollutants have killed the trees that held snow in place on slopes.

Treated snows

Snows on race courses are often treated, usually to ensure consistent conditions throughout a race day. The most common treatments are by water, chemicals and flame.

Watered snow is snow that has been sprayed with water, usually by a device resembling a garden sprinkler. The water sprayed on freezes to become ice, which stabilizes the snow. The patches sprayed usually are small relative to the overall size of a race course, and consequently require no change of waxing. The major problem they pose is that their icy surfaces make skiing difficult; not falling on a watered snow patch can sometime be a racer's greatest challenge.

Chemically treated snow: Chemicals can be sprayed on snow to elevate its melting point, so even though the air temperature may be well above 0°C (32°F), the effective snow temperature may be below freezing. Accordingly, waxing must be "colder." Chemical treatment is used mostly in the springtime, as race organizers or ski areas strive to retain snows as air temperatures rise. Summertime glacier ski areas sometimes chemically treat surface snow, to make it skiable through midday, when it otherwise would be turned to slush by the heat of the sun. However, since the chemicals used pollute runoff water, chemical treatment has been prohibited in many mountain regions.

Flame treatment is usually practiced on steeper sections of an Alpine race course which are expected to become pitted as racers ski by. Large, gas-fired torches are used to melt the snow surface, which is then allowed to freeze again. This binds the snow solidly to the underlying layers so that it resists pitting or gouging as racers ski by. Although flame treatment alters the snow, it has virtually no influence on the decisions made in waxing for an Alpine ski race, in which speed is more important on the flatter, straighter sections of a course than on its harder, steeper sections.

Brevity and inconsistency of directions

The instructions printed on a wax tube or can are your best guide to using a particular wax product. But their usefulness is limited, as they must be short, particularly when they are printed in several languages. Study all the instructions on all the containers of any one manufacturer, and you will probably find a few inconsistencies. In some cases, the same snow conditions may be described for differing products, or descriptions of conditions may differ from language to language on the same container. In some worst cases, temperature ranges differ from language to language. Errors such as these usually arise when products are updated or changed and put in production before all translations of the new directions are available and verified against the originals. Fortunately, most major wax manufacturers now have databases for directions, and common information, such as temperature ranges, is now printed in a large font at one place on a container.

FLUOROCARBONS AND HYDROCARBONS

The second generation of waxing, which began in the late 1940s, saw synthetic *hydrocarbons* become the ingredients of choice for ski waxes. The term "synthetic" means that the compounds involved are the products of chemical plants and are not found in their pure forms in nature. In the third and current generation of waxing, which began in the late 1980s, *fluorocarbons* both were used in new waxes and replaced some hydrocarbons in existing waxes. The term "synthetic" is not used in connection with fluorocarbons, because they are all manufactured. Synthetic hydrocarbon waxes glide better than do their natural counterparts, and fluorocarbon waxes glide better than hydrocarbon waxes. The differences in glide are due primarily to differences in **surface tension**; see that topic for further details.

Hydrocarbons

A *hydrocarbon* is a chemical compound that is composed only of hydrogen and carbon. As hydrocarbons are derived from petroleum, coal and plants, they comprise an enormous number of compounds. Accordingly, they are divided into three classes, *alicyclic, aliphatic*, and *aromatic*. The alicyclic hydrocarbons comprise molecules in which the hydrogen and carbon atoms join together to form one or more rings, and typical products made from them are alcohols, anesthetics and perfumes. The aliphatic hydrocarbons comprise molecules in which the hydrogen and carbon atoms join together in open chains. For skiers and snowboarders, they are the compounds of interest, as they include the chemicals from which plastics, such as polyethylene, and ski waxes are made. The aromatic hydrocarbons have a chemical structure similar to benzene (C_6H_6), in which carbon and hydrogen pairs link up in a regular hexagon, called a "benzene ring" Typical products made from aromatic hydrocarbons are styrene and phenol plastics and the ingredients of some motor fuels, particularly in Europe (*Benzin* is the German word for gasoline).

The refining of petroleum includes a process known as *dewaxing*, in which the hydrocarbons that solidify readily are separated from those that remain fluid at everyday temperatures. The hydrocarbons that solidify readily are the waxes; hence the name of the process. The waxes produced divide into two large families: *paraffin waxes* and *microcrystalline waxes*. The paraffin waxes comprise mixtures of 26 to 30 hydrocarbon compounds and melt at 45° - 62°C (113° - 144°F). Traditionally, one of the more common uses of paraffin waxes has been in candles. The microcrystalline waxes, named for their being built up of minute crystals, comprise mixtures of still greater numbers of hydrocarbon compounds and melt at temperatures up to 90°C (190°F). Both paraffin waxes and microcrystalline waxes are used as raw materials in ski waxes.

There is one exception to the prevalent use of synthetic hydrocarbons in waxing products. The volatile oils obtained from certain plants, including the wood of pine trees and lemon or orange citrus fruits, contain *terpenes*, a class of natural hydrocarbons which can be used to make solvents, including citrus-oil ski cleaners, another third-generation waxing product.

Fluorocarbons

The fluorocarbon compounds used in ski waxes are known as *per-fluorinated n-alkanes*. Translated from the language of chemists, that means that they are paraffin hydrocarbons - like propane and methane and other members of the aliphatic family whose members form the building blocks for hydrocarbon ski waxes - in which fluorine atoms have completely replaced the hydrogen atoms. In the paraffin waxes used in ski waxes, that's some 26 to 30 fluorine atoms per molecule. So you can think of fluorocarbon-based ski waxes as high-performance paraffins.

Fluorine, which sets fluorocarbons apart from hydrocarbons, has a mixed reputation. Its name comes from the Latin *fluo*, the root of words like "flow" and "flux," but meaning "unstable" when applied to a solid; the *ine* suffix means "pertaining to," from Latin via French. By itself, fluorine is a pale yellow, corrosive gas in which almost everything burns, including water. So in nature it never is found alone, but always with something else. And it is as abundant as are carbon, nitrogen or chlorine, and there is much more of it in the Earth's crust than copper or lead. Most commonly, fluorine is mated with calcium, in fluorite: the green, blue, purple, yellow or transparent crystals used for ornaments through the ages. Some of the most colorful rocks ever found are fluorite crystals on display at the American Museum of Natural History.

The properties of fluorine compounds were first observed in 1529, when they were used in fluxes. But more than three centuries passed before fluorine was first isolated by itself, in 1886. But that discovery did not lead to commercial production, as no use had been found for fluorine and no technology of the time could cope with its mean nature. Then came World War II and the development of the atom bomb, a project that required enormous amounts of fluorine. So safe and efficient production and transport methods were developed, and fluorine is now a readily available commercial chemical.

Mated with hydrogen, fluorine makes the acid that long has been used to etch the frosting on light bulbs. Mated with carbon and chlorine it fathers a family of chemicals known as the CFCs, whose inertness and stability led to a wide range of commercial and consumer applications, from aerosol propellants to refrigerants to fire extinguisher compounds. But, as we now know, released CFC gasses diffuse into the stratosphere, where ultraviolet light knocks off chlorine atoms that attack the ozone layer.

But fluorine can also be kind. It was in the water that led scientists to discover that fluoridation retards tooth decay. Although they are 19 times as heavy, fluorine atoms can replace hydrogen atoms in almost all hydrocarbons, resulting in materials with new properties and new uses. One is teflon, the tough, slippery plastic now used in coatings and in greaseless bearings. Another is in ski waxes.

So fluorine's dual social status is like that of hydrogen - which you cannot live without (in water), but which can be nasty (in acids), explosive (by itself) or totally lethal (in hydrogen bombs). Fluorine is both nasty and nice, depending on what you brew it with.

FRICTION

Skiers and snowboarders consciously or subconsciously rate glide on snow, sometimes with adjectives unfit for print. Yet glide on snow is far better than on any other common material. This is due to a unique combination of low shear strength (you pull some snow with you as you move over it) and high hardness close to its melting point (other materials soften before they melt).

All glide on snow involves overcoming resistance. This resistance is caused by air resistance, displacement of snow (pushing it aside), and friction (from the Latin *fricare*, to rub). Air resistance and snow displacement are familiar from other activities, which may be why they are so frequently discussed by skiers and snowboarders. Save for downhill ski racing and the inrun phase of ski jumping, air resistance is relatively unimportant for most skiers and snowboarders. For instance, at a downhill speed of 60 m.p.h., an average downhill ski racer or ski jumper on the inrun encounters an air resistance equal to about one-seventh body weight. At that speed, base-to-snow friction is about 30% as great as air resistance. At a speed of 35 m.p.h., the force created by friction on snow is equal to that of air resistance. At lower speeds, air resistance is progressively less than friction.

Although it opposes and consequently limits glide on snow, friction is indispensable. If there were no friction on snow, there would be no way to turn or control skis or snowboards. So almost all that can be said about glide can be expressed in terms of friction. Oddly enough, the worse the glide, the easier it is to understand. The scientific explanations of *static friction*, the standstill variety that permits the kick of classical cross-country, are straightforward. But the explanations of *kinematic (dynamic) friction*, important in explaining glide on snow, are more involved.

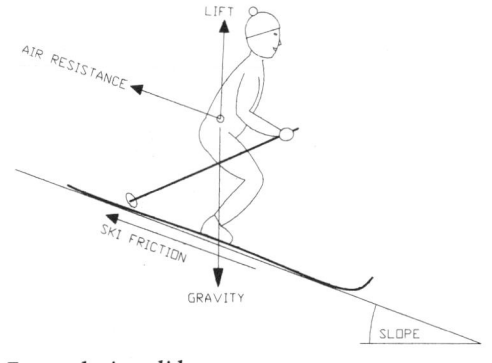

Forces during glide

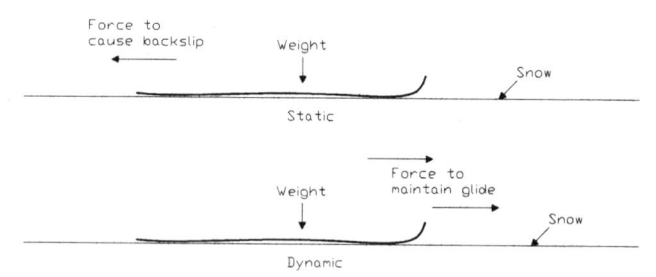

Static coefficient of friction determines grip in cross-country skiing; dynamic coefficient of friction limits glide of skis and snowboards

Many theories on dynamic friction have been put forth. All of them are complex, and not one of them is exactly right all the time, for all snows. But together two of them provide most of the answers related to skiing and snowboarding.

Dry friction

Dry friction is the sort explained in high-school science classes: the force to maintain motion of an object sliding over a surface is proportional to the weight of the object and the *coefficient of friction* between the object and the underlying surface. Dry friction resists sliding furniture across floors but enables you to walk. On snow, dry friction is most important at temperatures of -10°C (14°F) and below. The opposite of dry friction is *wet friction*, which occurs at the interface between a solid and a liquid. It is most important in boat building.

Mixed friction

Mixed friction (a mixture of dry and wet) occurs between two surfaces separated by a liquid. It is more complex than dry friction, because it depends also on the areas in contact and on the viscosity of the wetting liquid (viscosity is a liquid's internal resistance to flow). Under a ski or snowboard, the lubricating liquid is water. The question then is where does the water come from? Current scientific theory holds that there are four sources:

Friction melting is one of the older (dates from 1939) and by far the most quoted explanation of glide on snow. It contends that the friction of a surface gliding on snow produces enough heat to slightly melt the underlying snow particles, providing a water film (called "Bowden water") a few thousandths of a millimeter thick (few ten thousandths of an inch), which sustains glide. However, modern scientific computations have shown that the frictional heating under a ski or snowboard cannot account for the liquid that can sustain glide.

Pressure melting is similar to friction melting, save that the pressure exerted on the underlying snow is believed to melt the snow to provide a water film (called "Reynolds water") that sustains glide. Pressure melting is known to occur at almost all snow temperatures, which is one cause of the glaze on frequently used tracks and slopes. Pressure melting is most significant at temperatures just below freezing, -2° to 0°C (29° to 32°F). It is relatively small in skiing and snowboarding, but more important in ice skating and luge.

Microscopic atmosphere: A water layer (called "Faraday-Fletcher water"), about one angstrom (one ten millionth of a millimeter) thick, is found on the surface of all ice particles, due to the molecular structure of ice.

Meteorological effects include the actions of melt water, rainwater, and condensed water vapor.

Snow scientists know that neither dry friction nor mixed friction completely accounts for glide and that none of the known sources of lubricating water can supply all of it. The low effective coefficient of friction on snow is known to be due to the simultaneous actions of several effects, including deformation of the high points of snow crystals, plowing of particles rubbed off the snow surface, and adhesion between base and snow.

How small should the coefficient of friction be for good glide? How large should it be for a decent grip in classical cross-country? Questions such as these may be the wrong ones to ask, as numbers don't tell you what happens on snow. The way friction affects your ability to move on snow is what counts. Think, for instance, of the caveats in state driver's manuals and highway safety campaigns: vehicle stopping distance goes up with increased speed and up still more on wet or icy roads.

The coefficient of friction between good car tires and dry pavement is about 0.8, which limits vehicle braking distance at 55 m.p.h. to a minimum of 127 feet on a level road. Actual stopping distance is, of course, greater, as even the best brakes waste some stopping energy, and driver reaction distance adds to the total.

If the same road is wet, the coefficient of friction drops to 0.5, which ups the minimum braking distance at 55 m.p.h. from 127 ft to 203 ft. An icy road, with a tire-to-road coefficient of friction of 0.1, will further increase the minimum braking distance to 1020 ft.

In normal walking, you need a coefficient of friction of 0.2 or more between your feet and the underlying surface. If it drops to 0.1, you instinctively slow down, feel uneasy, and take shorter strides.

For gliding skis and snowboards, a coefficient of friction of 0.1 is moderate to poor; one of 0.05 is good. To see the difference, think of zipping downhill at 25 m.p.h. and coasting out onto a flat, evenly packed area of snow. With a coefficient of friction of 0.1, you'll stop in 210 ft. With a coefficient of friction of 0.05, you'll coast 420 ft. before stopping.

In these terms, the grip of classical cross-country skiing is still mostly glide, as a coefficient of friction of 0.4 is usually more than enough for most cross-country skiers. What's slippery for a car on a wet road is good snow bite for a cross-country skier. What's felt as slow under skis or snowboards is felt as disastrously slippery underfoot.

GLIDE WAXES

Glide waxes are available as pure hydrocarbon materials, mixes of hydrocarbon and fluorocarbon materials, or pure fluorocarbons (see **fluorocarbons and Hydrocarbons**) In general, the greater the fluorocarbon content, the better the glide and the higher the price of the wax. Wax manufacturers vary their hydrocarbon and fluorocarbon blends as they attempt to second guess what will serve skiers and snowboarders best. But they cannot be right on for all snows, for all skiers and all snow-boarders throughout the world, unless they produce glide waxes in an infinity of varieties to match all possible snow types. That's impossible. So, for top performance, some mixing is necessary (see **Mixing charts**). Physically, glide waxes are available in four forms:

Blocks of solid wax, which can be crayoned on and corked out for **Easy waxing**, or hot waxed for higher performance (see **Applying wax**). Glide waxes in blocks are available in a greater range of types, qualities, and prices than all other forms together. The types sold in ski and snowboard shops for individual use usually are square or rectangular blocks or sticks, with serrations, so convenient 20 gr (0.7 oz) smaller blocks can be broken off. Larger blocks, about 250 gr (about 9 oz) and chipped block wax in 3 kg (9 lb 6 oz) and larger containers, are used by ski shops in semi-automatic hot waxing machines.

Pastes are waxes liquefied by additive solvents so they have consistencies similar to those of toothpastes. They are available in tubes or tins, containing about 55 gr. (2 oz:) of paste, and in 1 kg. (2 lb. 3 oz.) cans. Single "portion" sachets, about 7 gr (1/4 oz), contain enough paste for one snowboard, the two Alpine skis of a pair, or two pairs of cross-country skis. Pastes are applied and let dry until the solvents evaporate. They can be used in **Easy waxing**, but are also the best substitutes for block waxes whenever you don't have enough time or equipment for hot waxing.

Liquids are wax compounds completely dissolved in solvents and are available in cans or plastic bottles, or as aerosols or pump sprays, containing various amounts of liquid. They are applied and let dry and are intended for **Easy waxing**.

Powders are high-performance fluorocarbon (see **Fluorocarbons and hydrocarbons**) waxes in their pure, granular form. They are usually available in small tins, fitted with salt-shaker type perforated tops and containing about 30 gr (slightly more than 1 oz) of powder. They are added after hot waxing and may be bonded hot or cold to the underlying wax.

GRIP WAXES

Grip waxes are available as pure hydrocarbon materials, mostly intended for recreational skiing, and in various hydrocarbon-fluorocarbon blends (see **Fluorocarbons and hydrocarbons**) intended for performance skiing and racing. In general, the higher the fluorocarbon content, the less a grip wax slows glide, the less it ices up, and the more it repels dirt. In terms of their consistencies, there are two main types of grip waxes for classical cross-country skiing, *hard waxes* and *klisters*, plus a hybrid called *klister-wax*.

Hard waxes: All dry-snow waxes and some wet-snow waxes of the **Easy waxing** two-wax systems come in foil cans containing about 45 - 50 gr. (about 1æ oz.) of wax.

Klisters (from the Swedish word for "paste") are tacky, thick liquids that appear and behave much like honey. Beware: they can be tricky if handled unskillfully; they can stick to hands, clothes, equipment - anything. But if you treat them with respect, they will behave beautifully on the wetter, more altered snows for which they are intended.

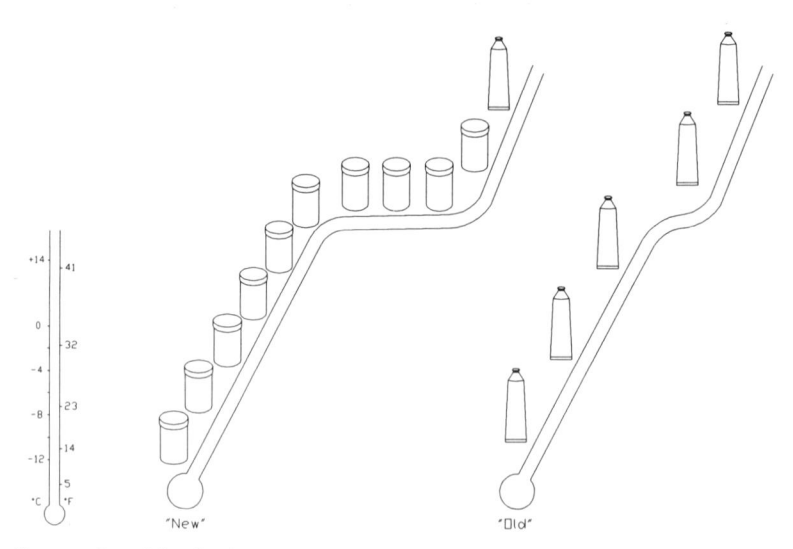

For exact match of grip wax to snow, you need many waxes, more hard waxes than klisters because new snow properties change radically at freezing.

Spray klisters are intended for **Easy waxing,** and consist of klisters dissolved in solvents in an aerosol spray can, fitted with a top sponge applicator. The applicator is pressed against a ski base to activate the spray, and then is used with less pressure against the base to spread the klister.

Klister-waxes look like hard waxes but behave somewhat like klisters, as they are intended for the tricky range of snow temperatures just above freezing.

Base binders are not pure waxes, but compounds aimed to reduce wear and tear and to adhere well to plastic bases and to wax. They come in small cans, as do the hard waxes, as well as in spray cans, and are intended to be used under grip waxes, to improve durability on abrasive snows.

HEAT

Beware!

Heat eases waxing; for high-performance waxing it's essential. But it's also easy to overuse. Aside from clumsy mistakes, like drilling straight through a ski or snowboard when mounting bindings, nothing damages as much as excess heat. So always be at least twice as careful as you think you should be when applying heat to bases.

Polyethylene, now nearly universal in bases, glides well partly because it is hydrophobic: it repels water. This property is a challenge in ski and snowboard manufacture, because glues and inks stick poorly to polyethylene. Consequently, the surface of a polyethylene sheet to be glued or printed is usually flame treated, because the oxidation produced vastly improves ink and glue adhesion. This is why the designs, logos, or lettering visible on polyethylene bases are actually silk-screen printed in reverse on the flame-treated surface of the transparent base sheet that is glued to the body of the ski or board.

The same oxidation that promotes glue and ink adhesion also permits water absorption, which defeats the hydrophobic property that gives polyethylene its good glide. Excess heat from a waxing iron or even excess sunlight can oxidize polyethylene. In the extreme, heat over 140°C (284°F) can melt polyethylene and irreversibly damage a base.

The telltale for incipient oxidation is color: chalk-white strips or patches signal its advance. If you see oxidation, scrape it off with a steel scraper, and prepare the base anew.

Sources

Flames, electric irons, and heat guns can be used in waxing and cleaning. Flames are too hot to be used directly on plastic bases, so you should use a flame to heat a hand-held waxing iron only when you have no electric outlet nearby. An ordinary household electric iron is one of the better sources of heat, as it can be adjusted to prevent overheating of a base plastic. Electric waxing irons, as available from major wax manufacturers, are usually made by household-iron manufacturers, and accordingly are equally easy to use and usually feature thermostat levels matched to waxing needs. Larger models, available from ski-machinery makers, are designed for continuous use and are recommended for technicians who work on many pairs of skis a day. Hot-air heat guns, are ideal for cleaning. But larger models, such as those intended to be flameless blowtorches, can produce as much heat as a hot torch flame, which is more than enough to damage bases; use them with caution.

Source	Temperature produced
Gas flame, of color:	
visible red	525°C (977°F)
orange	950°C (1742°F)
lemon yellow	1050°C (1922°F)
blue white	1400°C (2552°F)
Hair dryer	usually no more than 60° to 70°C (140° to 158°F)
Heat gun	usually adjustable in two or three steps, from a low of about 90°C (162°F) up to a high of 600° - 630°C (1112° - 1166°F)
Household iron:	
Low setting	100° - 110°C (212° - 230°F)
Medium setting	130° - 160°C (266° - 302°F)
High setting	up to 210°C (392°F)

Ventilate well when using a torch (see **Safety**). If you choose a heat gun, be sure to use one that can produce air-stream temperatures less than 200°C (392°F). For safety's sake in waxing, be sure that it conforms to the latest international requirement that if left running and placed on its side on a flat surface, it should not heat its surroundings by more than 60°C (140°F). The best models for waxing purposes come with a stand.

Hair dryers usually cannot put out enough heat for waxing purposes, but will do in a pinch. Don't hold the nozzle of a hair dryer close to a ski base. Most hair dryers have thermostats fitted in the blower tube behind the nozzle, to prevent singing hair. When the nozzle is held too close to an object, air flow is restricted, which causes air temperature to rise. The rise is sensed by the thermostat, which then cuts off the heat.

Use an ordinary household iron if you wish, but avoid a steam iron or an iron with a serrated sole that can collect wax. If you buy a new electric iron for waxing, be sure it is fitted with a fuse that cuts off the power to the heating element should the thermostat fail. This is particularly important in waxing, which is an application for which ordinary household irons are not designed. Vapors from waxes can damage an iron's thermostat, and a damaged thermostat can result in overheating of the base you are working on. If it fails, the sole of the iron can overheat seriously and, in a worst case of runaway heating, melt. Waxing irons available from wax manufacturers have all these features, and, in addition, have square or rectangular soles, well suited to waxing.

HINTS AND RULES

Skilled racers, waxing technicians and snow scientists often develop a sixth sense for snow and waxing. Here are some of the hints and rules that make up that sixth sense.

Always wax, even if you are "just a pleasure skier or snowboarder." Waxing not only ensures better glide, but also contributes to safety, as waxed and tuned skis and boards are easier to control in turns.

Be kind to bases: they may look tough, but they need tender, loving care.

Change seldom, particularly if you are a recreational skier or snowboarder and the weather is relatively stable. Yesterday's wax might work well today. But re-wax whenever wax on bases picks up dirt.

Do it indoors: wax indoors if you can; it's quicker and more comfortable.

Keep it simple: beware the overdo; spend your time on your skis or board, not waxing.

Keep notes on the waxing and base preparation that works best on the snows where you most frequently ski or snowboard. Nothing replaces local knowledge in judging snow.

Learn a lot about a few waxes; it's more experience, not more waxes, that makes you a better waxer.

Learn Celsius temperatures (sometimes called "Centigrade," meaning one hundred degrees). They're far more convenient for waxing than Fahrenheit temperatures: minus means dry snow, plus means wet snow, and zero is the borderline. The rest of the world, outside the USA, uses the Celsius scale, so knowledge of it is essential if you travel to snow abroad.

Less is best: more not only costs more, it usually works worse.

Let snow set the stage: it's what you are dealing with, and you cannot outsmart it. So learn it well.

Match well: easy methods for recreational skis and boards, high-performance methods for their high-performance and competitive counterparts.

Read the instructions on the wax can, tube, box or bag; they're your best guide to what's inside.

Remember carpentry: working on skis and snowboards is similar to cabinetmaking. Use implements that cut into bases, such as scrapers and sandpaper, as if you were using a fine plane. Work away from your body, pushing the blade or sanding block along the base, rather than pulling it to you.

Stick to one brand: that's enough; two brands make waxing twice as difficult.

When in doubt, wax hard: should you err, it's always easier to put a softer wax on top of a harder wax, both for glide and for the grip of classical cross-country. The other way round requires more effort.

Some tricks for classical cross-country ski grip:

Beware freezing: at 0°C (32°F), waxing is more difficult than at all temperatures above and below freezing. Don't expect to do well at it before you have gained some experience.

Beware nighttime weather: unless conditions are extremely stable, don't put on klister the evening before you intend to ski. An inch of new snow during the night is all that's needed to foil your plan to get out early. But if there isn't much new snow, you may master the situation; read on.

Reverse - sometimes: One of trickiest waxing conditions is hard tracks in older, more abrasive, granular snow, topped with a dusting of lighter, new, dry powder snow. Tracks often are set in the afternoon or evening for an early-morning race, and powder snow frequently falls during the night or in the morning. If you apply klister alone to match the snow in which the tracks were set, your skis will be slow, as the klister picks up new snow crystals and ices up. If you apply hard wax for the powder snow alone, you will find that you have no kick after a few kilometers, as the abrasive tracks wear the hard wax quickly. So compromise:

apply both klister for the hard tracks and a hard wax for the powder snow. Start with the klister, selecting and applying it as if the dry snow weren't there. Then cool your skis outside for half an hour or so. Select the hard wax that you would use on the powder, just as if the older snow weren't there. Apply it sparingly, covering the klister, and then smooth it out with a feathery touch of a waxing cork. This is the reverse of the general rule that hard wax shouldn't be put on top of softer wax. Cooling is the trick that permits it.

Risk slip, not stick: in waxing for snow at the critical freezing point, the main rule of waxing hard when in doubt holds doubly. If you wax your kick zones too hard, you may slip. If so, you can adjust by adding a softer wax. The opposite error is more serious. If you wax too soft, your kick zones will ice up and slow you to a standstill. Then the only way to change is to go back to the wax room, scrape your skis, and start over again.

When in doubt, shun klister: should the snow conditions seem to call for either hard wax or klister, choose hard wax. The lower the temperature, the more fortunate that choice. A hard wax on top of a base binder almost always is a more durable performer than a klister. But, as is the case for most rules, there is an exception; see **Reverse - sometimes** above.

HISTORY

An American start

In the 1860s, California gold rush miners held impromptu downhill ski races, complete with celebrations and prizes. They soon found that bases smeared with dopes brewed from vegetable and animal compounds helped increase skiing speeds. That started another race, to find the best dope, and many blends appeared, such as *Black Dope* and *Sierra Lightning*, which actually became a commercial product on a small scale. Its ingredients: 2 oz. sperm oil, 1/4 oz. pine pitch, 1/8 oz. camphor, 1 tablespoon balsam fir, and 1 tablespoon oil of spruce. Some enterprising miner-racers found that under certain conditions, paraffin candle wax worked well when melted onto ski bases. These are the events that started the art of glide waxing.

And in French it's...

In the 1890s, Norwegian inventor Emil Selmer (1864-1945) brewed a mixture of bronze powder and furniture polish to make the first ski wax to be sold internationally. He named it *fart* (Norwegian for "speed"), apparently with nary a thought of what the word meant in English. It soon dominated the market and was exported in quantity to Central Europe, primarily to France. The product became so popular that the French took its name to be generic. Hence two words in modern French, *fart* (ski wax) and *farter* (to wax skis). Norwegians are proud that these two words are among their few contributions to French. But the designers of multilingual wax packaging are less enthused, as French and English often must appear together.

The first generation

Though glide waxes were available at the turn of the century, the grip of classical cross-country skiing remained vexing. At very low temperatures, a smooth wood base would both grip and glide on snow. But as temperatures rose to or above freezing, snow moisture degraded both glide and grip. So, through the years, an amazing array of devices had been used to give skis grip. The oldest, a fur-based "kicker" ski dated from Viking times. The late 1890s saw the development of various fur strips and serrated wood and metal bases, most devised to both grip and glide, much like modern waxless cross-country skis. In 1913, Norwegian cross-country ski racer Peter Östbye (1887-1979) brewed the first tacky klister that gave good grip on wet and icy snows. That started a new era in grip waxing.

Glide and grip waxes then became true commercial products, available in ski shops. Up to the outbreak of the Second World War in 1939, dozens of brands appeared in Europe and North America, all brewed from animal and vegetable compounds, occasionally spiced with ground or melted phonograph records and bicycle inner tubes. These were the first generation of ski waxes, of which the most common ingredients included tar, tallow, stearin, linseed oil, rosin, beeswax, and paraffin wax, all natural compounds.

A Swede starts the second

In Europe, competitive skiing and most recreational skiing ceased during the Second World War, except in neutral countries, including Sweden. There, cross-country ski racer Martin Matsbo (1911-) reasoned that synthetic constituents were the secret to the future of ski waxes, as they were more amenable to industrial production techniques and quality control. Astra, the giant Swedish pharmaceuticals firm, agreed, and in 1943 gave Matsbo the go-ahead for the R&D needed. By 1946, the first waxes, three hard waxes and two klisters for cross-country skiing, were in production at Astra. Unlike their pre-war predecessors, they were made entirely of synthetic hydrocarbon compounds. They were also color-coded to ease selection. Matsbo's breakthrough waxes started the second generation of ski waxing. They also triggered the founding of Swix, an Astra subsidiary manufacturing company that subsequently changed hands and became a leading wax maker worldwide.

In the 1950s and 1960s, skiing, particularly Alpine skiing, grew rapidly. Led by the demands of racing, new technologies spawned new products, including metal (aluminum) and fiberglass skis with plastic bases, molded plastic boots, release bindings and poles with synthetic shafts. By the mid 1970s, ski equipment had caught up with waxes, so to speak, as almost all products were made of synthetic raw materials.

And Italians the third

Waxes had kept step with the developments, and convenient waxes for recreational skiing as well as high-performance waxes for racing were available for Alpine skiing, cross-country skiing, and ski jumping. Then, in the mid 1980s, two events in cross-country ski racing triggered a major change which was to affect all of skiing, as well as the then-new sport of snowboarding.

First, skating strides became accepted in racing and then split into a separate discipline called "free style." Because the force of a skating kick from an angled ski provided forward power, grip waxes were not needed in free style. So glide both became common to all of skiing and emerged as a major concern in cross-country World Cup racing. Cross-country skis are narrower than their Alpine counterparts, so they put greater pressure on snow, which in turn places a premium on accurate glide waxing.

So cross-country racers everywhere then sought faster glide waxes. The Italian racers were the first to be successful, with a fluorocarbon powder wax. Named *Cera* (Latin for "wax"), it was considerably faster, particularly at temperatures around freezing. By 1990, all major wax manufacturers had fluorocarbon waxes in their lines, which started the third generation in waxing. Fluorocarbon waxes are now available in various blends with hydrocarbon waxes (see **Fluorocarbons and Hydrocarbons**), for recreational and competitive Alpine skiing, cross-country skiing, ski jumping and snowboarding.

As wax manufacturers began compounding the third-generation waxes, snow scientists delved into new research on glide, both to explain why the fluorocarbons worked so well and to find optimum blends with hydrocarbon waxes, as the high cost of fluorocarbon raw materials would otherwise make them unaffordable for most skiers. The result was a new, more unified view of glide in which a base moving on snow interacts with it via an intervening interface. The branch of science involved is called **Tribology** (see that topic for details), and for skiers and snowboarders, the results have been a better understanding of the way bases and waxes work together on snow.

KICK ZONE

Classical cross-country ski strides require that a ski be waxed for both grip and glide. Recreational skiers may choose the truly classical approach and use cross-country grip wax only (see **Easy Waxing for classical cross-country**). But racers, as well as recreational skiers seeking top performance, *zone wax* by applying waxes where they are most effective: grip wax in the center of the base and glide wax ahead of and behind the grip wax. The area waxed for grip is called the *kick zone*, as it supports the kick of a stride. The areas waxed for glide are called *glide zones*.

The division into kick and glide zones is what separates performance waxing from easy waxing. It is useful only on performance skis, which have cambers that are stiffer than those of recreational skis. And a performance ski camber becomes stiffer as the ski flattens on snow, in a fashion similar to a multileaf truck spring becoming stiffer as the truck is loaded. The kick zones of the bases contact the snow slightly or not at all when the skis are equally weighted, as in downhill skiing or in gliding after double poling. The skis then glide on their glide zones. But when kicked down in a stride, the kick zone is pressed against the underlying snow. This characteristic is the reason why glide and kick zones can be waxed differently. The flip side of it is that if you don't have performance skis, there's no reason to performance-wax, as you cannot benefit from it. Kick-zone waxing is for high-performance recreational and racing skis.

Find the middle

The kick zone starts just under the heel of the boot or binding plate and extends forward about 16 to 20 inches, or about a third of the running surface of the base. On dry snows, most or all of the kick zone is waxed. On wet snows, particularly with klister, the kick zone is shortened by two to six inches at its front, to reduce drag.

Many performance skis have bases marked to indicate the location of the kick zone and interval distances within it. If your skis lack these marks, you must locate the kick zone. It isn't in the center of the ski, but rather in the center of the ski camber curve, which is located at different places on different skis. So you must test to find it. Ski manufacturers and shops do this with ski testers. But you can do almost as well by hand.

Hold a pair of skis vertically, bases together, and sight through the gap between the cambers as you squeeze the skis together

In classical cross-country, mid sections of skis are off snow during glide on two skis, but in contact with snow during kicks on one ski.

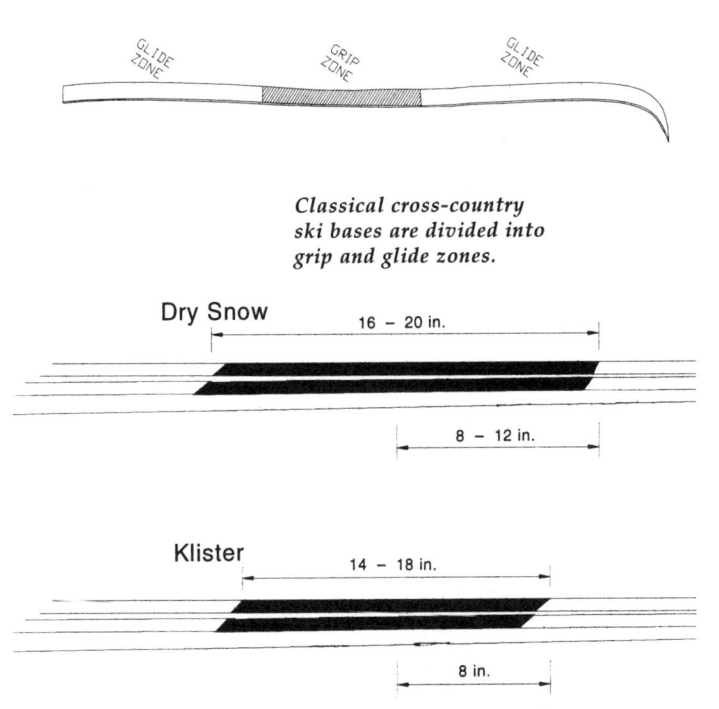

Classical cross-country ski bases are divided into grip and glide zones.

Dry Snow

16 – 20 in.

8 – 12 in.

Klister

14 – 18 in.

8 in.

Wax pocket for klister is shorter than for hard wax on dry snow

with your hands just behind the bindings (or, for new skis without bindings, with your hands just behind the balance point). when the gap closes down to about two feet, mark its front and rear points on both skis. The kick zone is between these marks.

Ski and see

How much of the kick zone you should wax depends on your skis, your proficiency and skiing speed, and on the snow and track conditions. The general rule is the stickier the grip wax, the less of it you need. There are two ways to find just how much. First, wax the bases entirely with cross-country grip wax. Then ski about three miles in abrasive snow tracks. Afterwards, examine wax wear. Where the wax has worn off most locates the glide zones. Where it has worn off least in the center of each ski locates the kick zones.

Second, do as racers often do before a start. Wax for the day as you think it will be: glide wax on the glide zones and grip wax on the entire length of the kick zone. Then, with a plastic scraper and a marking pen in your pocket or pack, test ski, to see if your skis have good grip. If they don't, you most likely have chosen the wrong grip wax. Go back to the wax room and re-wax. If they grip well, ski a bit, preferably about half a mile or so to let the wax "run in," and then stop and scrape off an inch or more of grip wax at the front of each kick zone. Then test ski again. Repeat the process until you have scraped grip wax to a point where the skis just slip. Mark this point; it is the forward edge of the *wax pocket* for the day's skiing. Finally, apply a bit of wax just in front of the mark (where you last scraped). Test again; you should have skis that grip and glide well.

Be wary in waxing

Never apply glide wax in the kick zone, as grip wax doesn't stick to glide wax. The only exception is just at the front of the kick zone, where you may either grip wax or glide wax, depending on the day's conditions. Note or mark your skis whenever you extend glide wax back into the front of the kick zone, and clean the area involved particularly well after skiing.

Sand the kick zones of your bases with #100 sandpaper to better the bond for grip waxes. Sand longitudinally, in the tip-towards-tail direction, until you see small, even striations in the base. Then buff with wiping tissue or scrape with a sharp plastic scraper to remove plastic fibers raised up from the base.

Always warm in the first layer of grip wax. After it has cooled, add two or three layers, smoothing each with a waxing cork. And always cork wax. Wax left rough may have better grip when you start skiing, but it will also slow glide. And as it wears smooth, its grip will diminish. If you need more kick, choose a softer wax. Many racers, who are experienced at waxing, take this maxim to an extreme. They pick one soft grip wax, usually one intended for use just below freezing, in the -2° to 0°C (28° to 32°F) range, and use it for even lower temperatures, as low as -10°C (14°F). The colder the snow, the shorter the "kicker."

MIXING CHARTS

The combinations of snow structure, snow source, air temperature, relative humidity, and the pressure under and speed of a waxed base moving on snow are infinite. But there's a practical limit to the varieties of wax that shops can stock and skiers and snowboarders can use.

So each wax product that you can buy in a shop is compounded by its manufacturer for an *ideal range* of snow conditions. Each range is described in terms of snow characteristics such as water content (dry or wet), age (new or old), consistency (fine-grained or coarse-grained), and temperature (a range in °C and °F). The general rule is that the newer and colder the snow, the harder the wax. Waxes for new, cold snow are the hardest; those for old, wet snow the softest.

At some point in its ideal range, each wax perfectly matches the snow; nothing performs better. But performance drops off toward the ends of its ideal range. In most cases, the ideal ranges of a single manufacturer's products overlap. In these overlapping parts of neighboring ranges, either wax may work. In most cases, a mix of the two neighbors works even better.

Manufacturers compound waxes for the worldwide average wintertime humidity of 60% in snow country and for average maximum skiing speeds. So humidities lower than about 35% call for harder waxes, while humidities over 85% call for softer waxes. Likewise, higher-speed events, like downhill and super-G, call for softer waxes, while events requiring greater turning accuracy, like slalom and giant slalom, call for harder waxes.

Classical cross-country skiers have long dealt with the needs for different amounts of ski grip, primarily by varying the length of the kick zone over which grip wax is applied. For glide, though, there is no equivalent simple answer, since all the area of the base that glides on snow must be waxed.

So mixing is the best way to ensure good glide whenever the ideal ranges of waxes overlap or humidities differ from the 35% to 85% ideal. The alternative, of course, would be to let the manufacturer mix for you. But then the number of waxes you would have to choose among - and buy to cover all contingencies - would at least quadruple. That would be impractical, both for you and for your ski or snowboard shop.

There are many ways to mix. For simplicity on one pair of skis or one snowboard, you can mix directly on the base, by

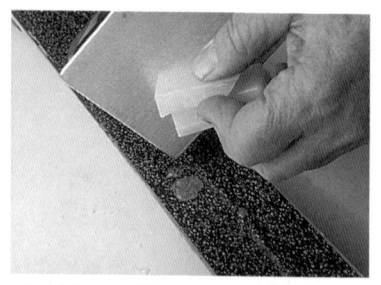

Hold two glide waxes against warm iron to mix down onto base

melting two waxes together on a waxing iron and then ironing them together on the base. Teams often prefer mixing in a small pot, heated on a stove or hotplate. *Mixing charts* are good guides to mixing proportions.

There probably are as many mixing charts as there are wax manufacturers and team technicians put together, and all are specific to particular product lines. Yet all share a common structure, which, for simplicity, can be illustrated by charts for a hypothetical line of three glide waxes, compounded for average wintertime humidity and skiing speeds:

S-wax is a soft wax for wet snow with a high percentage of free water.

M-wax is a medium wax for the -6° - +1°C (22° - 34°F) range.

H-wax is a hard wax for snows colder than -6°C (22°F).

S, M, and H each work well in their respective ideal ranges. But at the border between H and M and between M and S, their performance falls off. So mixing equal proportions of each of two waxes

°C	Rel. humidity 85% and higher		Normal humidity 35% -85%		Rel. humidity 35% and lower		°F
+6	S	S	S	S	S	S	41
+5	S	S	S	S	S	S	
+4	S	S	S	S	S	S	38
+3	S	S	S	M	S	M	
+2	S	S	S	M	S	M	35
+1	S	M	S	M	M	M	
0	S	M	M	M	M	M	32
-1	S	M	M	M	M	M	
-2	S	M	M	M	M	H	29
-3	M	M	M	M	M	H	
-4	M	M	M	H	M	H	26
-5	M	M	M	H	H	H	
-6	M	H	M	H	H	H	23
-7	M	H	H	H	H	H	
-8	M	H	H	H	H	H	20
-9	H	H	H	H	H	H	
-10	H	H	H	H	H	H	17
-11	H	H	H	H	H	H	
-12	H	H	H	H	H	H	14

Mixing charts for hypothetical three-wax line for high, normal, and low relative humidity

for these borderline ranges provides a better match to snow and effectively adds two waxes to the line. (Varying mix proportions would adds more varieties, but would also complicate this example, in which the mixes are assumed to be in equal proportions.)

These waxes are made for normal wintertime humidities. For humidites higher than normal, the mixes are softer, and for humidities lower than normal, the mixes are harder. So there are three mixing charts for humidities: normal, high, and low humidity. Likewise, waxes are made for average skiing speeds. So for each humidity range, there are mixing charts related to speed, such as one for downhill and super-G and one for giant slalom and slalom.

°C	Downhill Super-G		Giant Slalom Slalom		°F
+6	S	S	S	S	41
+5	S	S	S	S	
+4	S	S	S	S	38
+3	S	S	S	M	
+2	S	M	S	M	35
+1	S	M	S	M	
0	S	M	S	M	32
-1	S	M	S	M	
-2	S	M	M	M	29
-3	S	M	M	M	
-4	M	M	M	M	26
-5	M	M	M	M	
-6	M	M	M	H	23
-7	M	M	M	H	
-8	M	H	M	H	20
-9	M	H	H	H	
-10	M	H	H	H	17
-11	H	H	H	H	
-12	H	H	H	H	14

Mixing charts for hypothetical three-wax line for Alpine ski racing events

RILLING

New in skiing, old in the language

Rill is a word used since the early 16th century, as both a noun and a verb, to mean (noun) the small rivulets temporarily formed in soil or sand after rain or tidal ebb or (verb) to create rills. Any child who has ever built a castle in the sand of a seaside beach has probably seen it rilled and then washed away by incoming tide. Rills have long been a part of skiing, though this role was unrecognized until the 1980s.

In days of yore, all skis had longitudinal texture - rills in their bases - because all bases were made of wood oriented with its grain running lengthwise. But the effect of the rills went unnoticed. Although rills promote glide in wet snows, the wood bases absorbed water, which slowed skis and masked any advantages afforded by the natural rills. Then, in the mid 1980s, when skis had become all synthetic with smooth plastic bases, rills were rejuvenated to re-create their forgotten benefit in wood ski bases.

By chance, several snow scientists noticed that the design of ski bases for wet snows has much in common with boat building. Just as polished racing-boat hulls often are slower in the water than hulls with some longitudinal texture - which, some boat builders maintain, is why wood boats sometimes beat fiberglass boats in races - perfectly smooth, correctly waxed ski bases are often slow in wet snow. Skiers had felt the effects of this slowness ever since the first plastic bases had appeared in the 1950, and had named it *suction*, because the skis felt as if they were sucked down into the snow, like two wet panes of glass sticking to each other. So the cure for plastic-based ski slowness

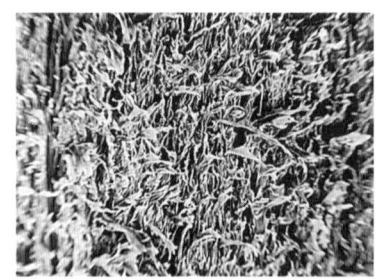

Surface of new base has microscopic burs (100X magnified)

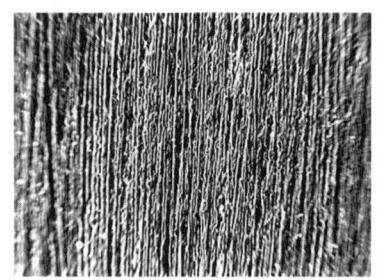

Rilling removes microburs and imparts longitudinal microgrooves (100X magnified)

is the same as for boat slowness: longitudinal grooves, or *rills* in the base improve water flow and thereby improve glide.

The American connection

Rilling leapt into the headlines in 1987, although it had been practiced in skiing for several years. That year the *Stars and Stripes* yacht won back America's Cup by outsailing its Australian rival. The win was partly attributed to grooves applied to the hull of the *Stars and Stripes*, with *riblet* (means "small rib") tape, which comprises rows of small isosceles triangles about 1/64 in. high. The tape had been developed by the 3M Corporation in St. Paul, on the basis of NASA experiments showing that grooves reduced drag on airplane wings.

For wet and dry

Although rilling of ski bases evolved from the need to drain water from under the base on wet snows, it has an equally important mission on dry snows, for which rills can be cut in patterns that retain water. The general rule is, then: coarse pattern to let water flow out on wet snows, and a fine pattern to retain water on dry snows.

Alpine skis and Telemark skis

Wax manufacturers offer bronze and steel brushes of various bristle size and spacing, for both coarser and finer rilling of bases (see **Tools**). Fix a ski firmly in a waxing horse or a set of waxing vises, base up, before brushing. If you hold the ski by hand, your brush may wander and gouge uneven rills that fail to work as they should. See **Base preparation** for rilling techniques. Rilling can also be done as part of the **stone grinding** done in well-equipped repair shops; see that topic for further details.

Cross-country skis

Wax manufacturers offer rilling tools with interchangeable toothed irons (see **Tools**). Note that these tools cannot be used on Alpine skis or Telemark skis, which have steel edges. The *pitch* (distance measured between the midpoints of adjacent teeth) of the irons varies; the three most common pitches are: fine, 0.5 mm (slightly more than 1/64 in.) for dry snows; medium, 0.75 mm (about 1/32 in.) for all snows; and coarse, 1 mm (slightly less than 3/64 in.) for wet snows. Pitches down to 0.25 mm (slightly

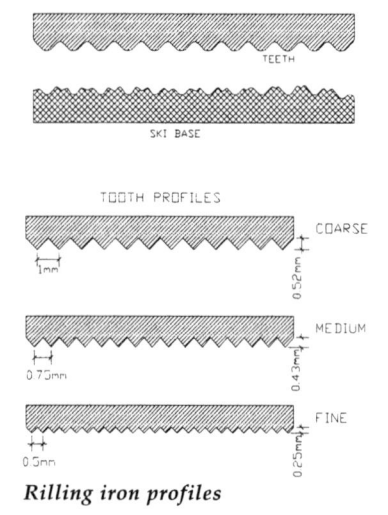

Rilling iron profiles

less than 1/100 in.) and up to 3 mm (about 7/64 in.) are also available. A rilling iron is fixed in a holder, which is shaped to fit the hand and has guides that slide along the ski sides. Fix a ski firmly in a waxing horse or a set of waxing vises, base up, before rilling, because even with its guides, a rilling iron is hard to control on a hand-held ski. See **Base preparation** for rilling techniques.

SAFETY

The first safety rule for all waxing and working on skis or snowboards can be stated in one word: **ventilate!** Manufacturers strive to make their products safe in use, but there are practical limits to just how safe a product can be: even ordinary flour can explode if there is enough of it in the air of a poorly ventilated room. An open window and an exhaust fan can do wonders, just as they can in a kitchen when you want to prevent the smells of cooking from permeating the house. Be particularly aware of the potential hazards in using epoxy, fluorocarbon waxes, base repair tools, solvents, and gas torches.

Epoxy

The US Public Health Service regards epoxy resins and hardeners as occupational health hazards. So always observe the safety rules for epoxy use, even if you use only small quantities, such as a two-component epoxy filler or glue for ski or snowboard repair. In short, the PHS guidelines advise keeping all epoxy materials away from your mouth and eyes, keeping all fire and sparks away from fumes, ventilating well to prevent inhaling vapors, and being meticulous in cleaning up and washing your hands after using epoxy compounds. If you frequently do your own repairs using epoxy compounds, take a tip from professional repairmen, and buy and wear a pair of industrial-grade rubber gloves for the task. Ordinary household rubber gloves won't do, as epoxy can attack the materials of which they are made.

Fluorocarbons and base plastics

Fluorocarbons react with few other substances, so they usually are as safe to handle as conventional ski waxes. But you should be aware of the potential hazards, in order to avoid them.

Beware heat: it brings out badness. At high temperatures, 300°C (570°F) or above, fluorocarbons may decompose. Inhaling the fumes of decomposition can cause *polymer fume fever*, also called the *teflon shakes*, an illness with symptoms similar to the occupational fevers suffered by welders and other metalworkers who inhale volatilized metals. So don't smoke and don't use open flames when working with fluorocarbon waxes. For most skiers and snowboarders, the chimera is easily kept at bay: flames are out when working with polyethylene ski bases.

Avoid dust: small particles of any wax, hydrocarbon or fluorocarbon, or plastic base material can irritate your nose, throat, and lungs if inhaled. So if you work with wax or bases for longer periods, or if you use power brushes or buffers, wear a particle filter mask. A disposable paper mask, as used in woodworking and spray painting, is usually adequate. But should you notice irritation or know that you are particularly sensitive to dusts, wear an industrial-type respirator mask with a dust filter.

Elude fumes: plastic fumes, as given off by burning base repair "candles" and heated base-welding tools, are noxious. So, for safety's sake, wear a respirator mask fitted with an organic-vapor filter.

Solvents

Never use highly flammable solvents, such as acetone, gasoline, or lighter fluid, to remove wax or clean skis. But even the most benign wax solvents are flammable, so always read and heed the flammability caveat on the label. And read the toxicity statement on any solvent you buy; avoid those that are toxic. The biodegradable citrus-oil solvents available from wax manufacturers are your safest bet.

Wear rubber gloves when using solvents, both to keep the solvent from removing the oil in your skin and to keep your hands clean, as wax removal can be messy.

Always dispose of wax- or solvent-soaked rags or cleaning tissue in a safe place, preferably a fireproof rubbish can with a lid.

Keep your work area clean, so you can see any spilled solvent or blobs of wax. Always clean up your work area after cleaning your skis or snowboard.

Gas Torches

If you use a gas torch, use a welder's spark lighter to light it. Avoid matches and cigarette lighters, as they may continue to burn after you have lit a torch. Light your torch as quickly as you would light a gas stove, for the same reason: escaping gas is noxious and can explode. Always direct a torch flame away from your body, and ensure that there is a large open space behind it. Using a torch on a workbench littered with wax, rags and junk invites disaster.

If you fly to snow and take your wax torch along, leave its gas containers behind, as both federal and international aviation-safety regulation prohibit their transport on passenger aircraft. The reasons for the ban are sound. Seals on gas-torch refill containers as well as on disposable containers are intended to contain the gas when there's normal air pressure outside and the containers are undamaged. But when the outside air pressure drops, as it does in an airplane, or when a container is damaged, as it might be if baggage bounces about, a container can leak and turn an aircraft into a flying bomb. Accordingly, federal regulations are strict: a violation can result in a fine or imprisonment. Warnings to this effect are required to be posted by airlines. So if you take a torch on a flight, select one that runs on commonly available refills, such as the propane flasks sold in hardware stores throughout North America. The torch-head valve unit is harmless; only gas is grounded.

SNOW

Snow sets the scene, wherever and whenever it occurs. Poets and painters have long praised its beauty. But to many who must cope with its effects, it is an undesirable, expensive nuisance: winters are often remembered for the havoc of their blizzards, particularly in cities that see snow so infrequently that they are unprepared for it.

The peoples of the north have lived with snow for centuries. Yet historically, snow and cold have both hindered colonization of northern areas and thwarted armies (Hannibal, Napoleon, Hitler), events which in turn changed history. Major team sports, such as football in the USA and soccer in Europe, often suffer when autumn games are canceled by early snows. Yet winter sports depend on snow and cold. For those who deal with it, snow has a far greater impact than any other aspect of wintertime weather.

Consequently, snow long has been studied by scientists. The first on record was Olaus Magnus (1490-1557), Archbishop of Uppsala, Sweden, who lived mostly in Italy after 1530 and compiled the monumental *Historia de gentibus septentrionalibus* (History of the Nordic peoples), published in Rome in 1555 and containing the first known descriptions and illustrations of snow. Meteorologists now study snow as part of the weather cycle; hydrologists study snow because it supplies a third of the water used for irrigation worldwide; glaciologists study snow to understand glacial buildup; and chemists study means of snow and ice control, such as salting and sanding city streets. Considerations of snow are important in other fields: building engineers compute the snow loads on structures; highway and road engineers design slopes and shoulders to deal with snow and frost heaves; and mechanical engineers design snow plows, snow-packing machines, and, of course, ski lifts. Loosely, the sectors concerned with snow in all these fields are together known as the *snow sciences*, so a *snow scientist* is a person concerned with finding out more about snow. All considerations of snow divide into two major groups: *snow in the atmosphere* (snow formation and snowfalls) and *snow on the ground* (buildup, existence and final run-off of snow cover).

Snow in the atmosphere

Rain and snow come from clouds, as everyone knows. The more exact scientific statement is that precipitation can occur whenever there is a surplus of moisture in the atmosphere. When the temperature is sufficiently low, that precipitation can be in the form of snow. The imprecision of that scientific statement is deliberate, because there are so many variables in the meteorological recipe for snow that even the main variable, temperature, gives only an incomplete picture. Under certain (and complex) conditions, rain may be *supercooled,* a condition in which it is below freezing but remains liquid.

Just as rain drops come in different sizes, all snow crystals start small and then grow. Each snow crystal begins its life as a minute ice crystal, usually six-sided and no larger than 0.075 mm (0.0003 in.), in its greatest extent. As soon as it is formed, it starts to fall towards the ground below. It falls slowly at first, about one foot a minute. Water vapor then sticks to it, in a process known as *sublimation,* and it gradually grows, until it becomes a larger crystal that can be seen by the unaided eye. Individual snow crystals may stick together, as in a heavy snowfall at temperatures near freezing, to form larger snowflakes. Snow crystals often fall through layers of air containing supercooled water droplets, which freeze on their surfaces as *rime* (deposited frost). By the time these crystals reach the ground, their original shapes may be totally obliterated.

Snow crystals develop differently, depending on the temperature and moisture prevailing in the clouds where they are formed and on the conditions in the layers they pass through on their way to the ground. The result of all these variations is that no two falling snow crystals are exactly alike. But they can be classified into groups with beautifully descriptive names, including: *plates, stellar crystals, columns, needles, stellar forms in three dimensions, capped columns with plates on ends or sides,* and *irregular shape (not possible to classify).*

Snow on the ground

Snow crystals are among the most unstable structures in nature; they begin to change as soon as they are deposited on the ground, due to processes known as *metamorphism* (meaning change of form and due to mechanical forces. They can also change before they hit the ground, as when wind packs them together in the air.

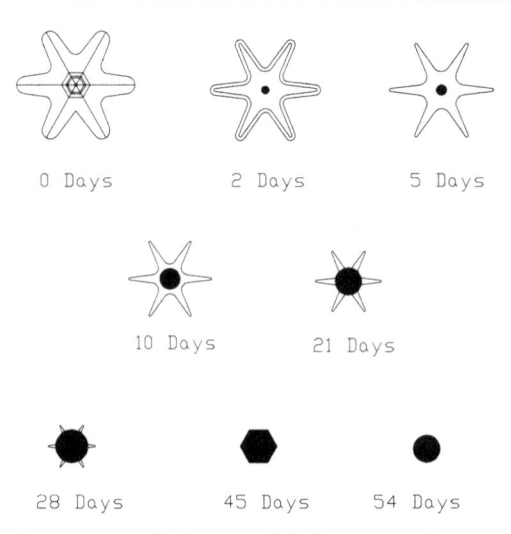

A snow crystal changes with time, even when temperature and humidity remain constant.

The complexities boggle. In one respect, snow on the ground is more easily described than snow in the atmosphere, as there are fewer types of particles. However, the only thing completely certain about any classification of snow on the ground is that with time it will be different, because snow on the ground changes relentlessly.

So in the course of a winter, snow cover builds up in layers of varying thickness, hardness, and structure. The characteristics of each new snow layer depends on the crystal structure of the snow that fell and on the weather that prevailed thereafter. A layer of snow can be thought of as porous, like a giant sponge. The snow surface and the underlying layers consist of solid water (ice) in an irregular, skeleton-like structure. The cavities are filled with air and water vapor, which circulate among the ice and snow particles. The size of the cavities, or *pore volume*, indicates the density of the snow, or how hard it is packed. Ice crystals and water vapor exist together when the air is cold and the snow is dry. Water, called *the liquid state* to distinguish it from ice (solid water), may be bound in ultrathin films, barely a few molecules thick, on ice and snow particles, or be not bound but free to move among ice and snow particles, under the influences of capillary forces or gravity. The presence of free water depends on conditions for melting; in which the snow cover or a part of it reaches its maximum temperature of 0°C (32° F).

Density, or weight per unit volume, is an important characteristic of snow on the ground. However, for skiers and snowboarders, qualities like age, moisture content, snow crystal size, hardness and shape are of prime concern. All of these characteristics change continually, through metamorphism and under the influence of mechanical forces.

At temperatures below freezing, *destructive metamorphism* is the chief cause of alteration. It is named for its principal action, which destroys the delicate structures of new snow crystals. A new snow crystal has many fine, sharp points and edges, and is surrounded by water vapor. Because the pressure is higher on the sharper, more pointed parts of the crystal than on its more rounded parts, the sharper points are eroded as water vapor is transported away. This rounds off all sharp surfaces, and the crystal gradually assumes its final, stable, spherical shape. So the snow crystals in a layer of new, fluffy snow gradually diminish into little balls and become more densely packed; that's when the snow is said to be "old." Temperature determines the speed of this process. The higher the temperature the more rapid the aging of the snow.

At temperatures above freezing, *melt-freeze metamorphism* takes over as the prime process of change. It depends on there being free water in the snow. So it is most common in late winter or spring, and otherwise may occur at any time during the winter, whenever air temperature rises above freezing.

The free water may come from melted snow or from rain falling on the snow cover. Rain can increase snow moisture content considerably, but contrary to popular opinion, rain plays only a minor role in the melting of snow. Melting just one gram (about 1/28 oz.) of snow requires 80 calories of heat (the calorie of high-school science, not the dietary calorie, which is one thousand times larger). Rain at a few degrees above freezing lacks the heat energy for the job.

Changes caused by repeated melting and freezing are most common in late winter, when daytime sun melts snow and sub-freezing nighttime cold refreezes it. The first melt of a snow layer changes it radically, by causing it to sink, as many of its pores fill with water. The warming first melts the smaller crystals, and then the melt water fills the spaces between the larger crystals and, in turn, alters their surfaces. That's the simple part. The rest is complex.

When the melt water trickles downwards, it can refreeze at a lower level. A snow cover can retain a considerable amount of water if it melts slowly. The speed of melting depends on the temperature and its variation throughout the snow cover. Melting is fastest when the entire snow cover is isothermal at 0°C (32°F). The pores then fill with water; the snow cover is said to be mature, and it starts to run off as water.

Mechanical forces also enter the picture in new snow layers composed of dry-to-moist snow crystals. New snow crystals fall, on top of the others, to build snow cover. As the layers of snow build up, the increasing weight of the crystals on top crushes the lowermost crystals. Wind compounds crushing, as it drives crystals into each other. Crystal shape also plays a role: the most delicate, star-shaped crystals are the most subject to damage. So great are the forces of wind that wind-driven snow can break down even before reaching the ground. Nearer the ground, new snow from above and old snow from below mix and swirl together, eradicating the differences between them. The wind-driven snow crystals bump into and rub against each other, causing damage and wear. These effects of wind explain why new, wind-driven snow is denser than it otherwise might be at the same temperature. And the greater the density, the greater is the contact area between snow and the gliding base of a ski or snowboard, and the greater the friction. This is why windpack is always slow.

SNOW TYPES

Snow can be classified in many ways and indeed is, by snow scientists and on-line snow report writers alike. The classifications in widespread use in snow sports worldwide type snow according to its grain character, wetness and hardness.

Grain character

With some variations, ski and snowboard wax manufacturers describe snow in terms of three categories of grain character:

New snow: falling or newly fallen snow that has not yet changed on the ground.

Fine-grained snow: older snow on the ground, with its crystals rounded.

Coarse-grained snow: snow on the ground that has gone through one or more freeze-thaw cycles, so the individual grains have formed larger grains.

Wetness

The international terminology of the snow sciences defines five categories of wetness, in terms of free water content of the snow. Most wax manufacturers use these categories in designing waxes and in writing directions for their use.

Dry: Snow usually, but not necessarily, below 0°C (32°F). The individual grains of the snow stick poorly to each other when squeezed in a gloved hand.

Moist: Snow at 0°C (32°F), with no water visible (to unaided eye or eye aided by an ordinary hand lens). When squeezed in a gloved hand, the snow makes a snowball.

Wet: Snow at 0°C (32°F). Water is visible between the grains, but it cannot be pressed out of a snowball squeezed in a gloved hand.

Very wet: Snow at 0°C (32°F). Water can easily be pressed out of a snowball squeezed in a gloved hand. The snow still contains a large amount of air.

Slush: Snow at 0°C (32°F). The snow is sopping wet; it is full of water and contains very little air.

Hardness

Snow hardness is classified in various ways, most involving quantities that require scientific instruments to measure. Fortunately, the simple hand test gives results adequate for most purposes, including skiing and snowboarding. In it, snow hardness is classified according to how small and sharp an object need be to leave an impression in the snow when poked into it by hand.

Hardness classification	Largest object that can leave impression when poked into snow by hand
Very soft snow	Fist
Soft snow	Four fingers
Medium hard snow	One finger
Hard snow	Sharp pencil
Very hard snow	Knife
Ice	Ice pick

STONE GRINDING

The grinding machines that ski manufacturers and fully equipped ski-repair shops use to finish Alpine ski bases are built for their purpose, but otherwise resemble their sibling machines used by machine shops to work metal. They are called *stone grinders* because their abrasive grinding wheels are made of natural or artificial stone, which is *dressed* in the machine. Stone grinding is used both to flatten bases that are railed or bowed and to cut patterns that aid either stability or turnability.

A typical stone grinder has a flat table, or *bed*, at a convenient working height. The stone rotates about an axis parallel to and beneath the bed, so its surface protrudes through a guarded opening above the bed. A diamond cutter is usually fitted to travel across the surface of the stone, to *dress* it and thereby produce the variations in its surface that impart various structures to the bases that are ground. Dressing is seldom used in grinding railed or bowed bases to make them flat. The ski is guided over the revolving stone and held base-down against it by a *feed* wheel, which is a rotating roller with a soft surface that grips the top of the ski and pulls it forward. The stone speed, stone structure, feed speed and grinding pressure determine the final finish produced.

Stone speed: The effective stone speed is actually the speed of the periphery of the stone that grinds the base. But it usually is expressed in revolutions per minute (r.p.m.) of the stone. The higher the r.p.m., the faster the stone works the base, and the more material it removes in each pass of the ski over it. However, excess speeds can heat bases unduly, causing oxidation or, worse, burning and melting.

Stone structure: In general, the coarser the stone, the more material it removes in each pass of the ski through the grinder. If the diamond dressing cutter moves slowly with respect to the stone speed, the stone cuts fine structures in the base. If it moves faster, the stone cuts coarser structures in the base. The two types of structures cut into bases are *linear structures* and *cross structures*. Linear structures resemble dashed lines longitudinally along the base and are cut to improve stability at speed and to retain water under the base, as often needed on cold, dry snows. Cross structures resemble sequences of X-shaped crosses along the base and are cut to aid turning and to help remove water under the base, as often needed on wet snows.

Feed speed determines how fast the base goes past the spinning stone. The lower the feed speed, the more material is removed from the base in each pass. The higher the feed speed, the less material is removed in each pass and the less is the chance of overheating. For any fixed stone speed, the faster the feed, the longer is the repetitive structure cut in the base and the more the structure aids ski stability. The slower the feed, the shorter the structure and the more the structure aids turning.

Grinding pressure affects the amount of material removed in each pass and the depth of the pattern cut into the base. The greater the pressure, the more material is removed and the deeper the pattern cut. Deeper patterns aid ski stability, while shallower patterns aid turning.

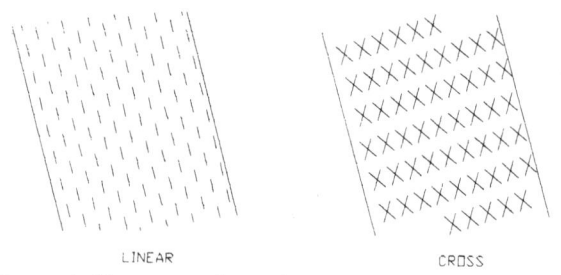

LINEAR   CROSS

Stone grinding can produce a linear or a cross pattern

SURFACE TENSION

Through the years, the gliding of skis on snow has mystified scientists and skiers alike, as no one theory explains the whole. But snow scientists now agree that surface tension - the property that causes the concave curvature, or meniscus, of a column of water in a vertical tube - plays a prime role, as it determines how much force must be applied to move something over the surface of a substance. The lower the surface tension, the more slippery the substance.

Water itself is fairly slippery; not many common substances outdo it. As shown in the bar chart, one is polyethylene, the plastic used on ski and snowboard bases: it has a surface tension less than half that of water. Acetone, as used in nail polish remover and some glues, comes in at a third, as do the hydrocarbon compounds used in ski waxes. Teflon is even more slippery, with a surface tension one quarter that of water. But the fluorocarbon compounds used in third-generation ski waxes beat even teflon, with a surface tension one fifth that of water. Few common compounds beat them. One is dry ice (solid carbon dioxide), which theoretically would be great under skis or snowboards - if you could find suitable snow and a way to stay comfortable at the ultra-low temperatures, below -78°C (-109°F) at which it remains solid.

Water	0.075
Polyethylene Ski Base	0.030
Acetone	0.026
Hydrocarbons in Ski Waxes	0.025
Teflon	0.020
Fluorocarbons in Ski Waxes	0.015
Dry Ice	0.009

Surface tensions of slippery compounds compared to water (as measured in the international metric system of units of Newtons per meter)

TEMPERATURE

Two temperature scales are in common use, the Fahrenheit scale, used in the USA but now being phased out in the rest of the English-speaking world, and the Celsius scale, uniformly used elsewhere worldwide. The numbers on the scales are historical choices, which have been difficult to define accurately in the light of modern scientific knowledge.

Fahrenheit scale

The scale is named for Gabriel Daniel Fahrenheit (1686-1736), a German physicist who lived most of his life in the Netherlands and in England and made his living making meteorological instruments. He was the first to use mercury instead of spirits of wine for thermometers. He also constructed a temperature scale, for which the zero point was the temperature of a mixture of ice and common table salt. Initially he elected to subdivide the interval between that temperature and the body temperature of a healthy adult into 12 equal units, but subsequently increased the number of units to 96. On his scale, 0 then was the temperature of his mixture of ice and salt, and 96 was the temperature of the human body. The convenience of the scale, he believed, was that the freezing point of water was at 32, which would avoid negative numbers in expressing temperatures (apparently he knew of no lower temperatures) and that the human body temperature was stable. Subsequently, the average human body core temperature was found to be higher, 98.6°, and the temperature of a mixture of ice and common table salt was found to vary. Nonetheless, Fahrenheit's scale was adopted, particularly in English-speaking countries. It was long favored by meteorologists, as it had smaller degrees than other scales.

Celsius scale

The scale is named for Anders Celsius (1701-1744), a Swedish astronomer and professor at Uppsala. He was the first to see the convenience of a temperature scale having one hundred divisions with its zero and one hundred degree points at the freezing and boiling points of pure water at sea level. The scale gained acceptance throughout Europe, and was favored by scientists for its arithmetic convenience. At the General Conference of Weights and Measures held in 1927, the US National Bureau of Standards and equivalent agencies in England and Germany proposed the *International Temperature Scale*, a scientifically accurate version of the Celsius scale. It was accepted by the representatives of 31 nations at the Conference. It's zero and one-hundred degree points were precisely defined respectively as the *ice point* and the *steam point* of pure water. That scale became known as the *Centigrade scale*, as it had one hundred degrees. Subsequently, it was even more accurately defined. The new definitions superseded those of 1927, and the scale was named *Celsius*, in honor of its originator. Its zero and one-hundred degree points differ only by a few hundredths of a degree from those of the centigrade scale. So for practical purposes, the Celsius scale, now the accepted international name, and the centigrade scale may be considered identical.

Conversion

Do you remember all that dividing (or was it multiplying?) by nine (or was it five?) that you learned in school science classes? Confusing, to say the least. It's better to remember a few temperatures and work from there.

Fahrenheit to Celsius: First subtract 32, then divide by 2 and add 10 percent. *Example*: What's 50°F, a warm winter temperature, in degrees Celsius?

$50° - 32° = 18°$ above freezing
$18° \div 2 = 9°$
$9° + 10\%$ of $9° = 9.9°C$
which is nearly right; the accurate figure is 10°C.

Celsius to Fahrenheit: First multiply by 2 and subtract 10 percent, then add 32. *Example*: What's -10°C, a common temperature stated for waxes, in degrees Fahrenheit?

$-10° \times 2 = -20°$
$-20° - 10\%$ of $-20° = -18°$ below freezing
$-18° + 32° = 24°F$
which is right on.

For an additional crutch, remember a few temperatures, also useful should you travel abroad: 98.6°F, the human body temperature, is 37°C. A comfortable indoor room temperature is 72°F, or 20°C.

TESTING GLIDE

Classical cross-country ski racers know that the grip, or "kick," of a pair of skis is individual, because skier weight and gait are as decisive as wax choice and application. To a degree, the same can be said of glide for all skiing and snowboarding. It is crucial in all racing, which is why teams frequently test glide before races. But it remains partly individual, which is why a pre-race glide test cannot be an absolute indication of the best waxing for the day.

The principles of testing are best illustrated by the testing procedures evolved by major ski teams. The first step is selecting the skis to be tested.

The properties of skis can vary considerably, sometimes so much that they affect the outcome of a test more than the way a ski is waxed. This is why major ski teams always have four or five pairs of test skis that are as nearly identical as possible. The skis selected are of the same make, model and length, and come from the same production run in the same press, with their bases made of plastic from the same strip of material. Their cambers have been tested and found equal. On the test day, the same person waxes all pairs to be tested, using the same methods and tools. These precautions are necessary to ensure that the test is of waxes and waxing methods, not of skis.

The skis are then waxed and test-skied over a marked, straight downhill track or slope. Runs are timed from a start mark to a stop mark, preferably using an electronic photocell timer of the type used to time races. The distance between the start and stop marks ideally should be long enough that the skiing time between them is 10 to 20 seconds. At cross-country ski-racing speeds of up to 18 m.p.h., the test distance is then about 270 to 540 feet. At downhill ski racing or inrun ski jumping speeds of up to 60 m.p.h., the ideal test distance of about 880 to 1760 feet is too long to be practical in pre-race testing. Consequently, high-speed tests are usually made through a zone on a course or a ski jump inrun, with timing accurate to thousandths of a second.

Several runs are made with each pair of skis, and skiers switch skis after each run so that each test skier skis on all pairs during a test. Many runs with a few pairs of skis are always preferable to few runs with many pairs of skis, because with fewer pairs, the differences between them can more easily be eliminated from the test results. Five runs and four or five pairs of skis are adequate to give meaningful data on glide. All tests should be made as quickly as possible, to rule out the effects of changing snow conditions. Variations in wind from test to test can degrade the accuracy of results. So wind speed, as measured by a portable or nearby fixed anemometer, is usually noted, as is air temperature. Timing is arranged in the same manner as for a race. A timer notes the time of each run against the test racer's number and ski pair-number. The test racers' numbers are important in the subsequent analyses, to eliminate the human factor from measurements. Some racers, for instance, can more consistently ride a flat ski than others, and hence glide faster in test skiing.

The first test is of pairs of skis that are identically waxed, to measure any differences between them. A typical test on cross-country skis might produce results like these:

Pair number	Average of five timed runs, seconds
1	18.91
2	18.30
3	18.01
4	18.24

Thus, although the skis were chosen to be as identical as possible, there are small differences among them. For instance, pair number 3 is faster than pair number 1 by about 5%. Consequently, in the following tests of different waxes, a 5% handicap will be added to pair number 3 times in comparing them with pair number 1 times.

The test is then repeated, with the skis waxed differently. The results of tests conducted at as nearly identical wind speed and air temperature as possible are selected for comparison. After the handicap times of the first test are added, the final results can be assessed to find the fastest waxing for the day.

TOOLS

In alphabetical order, the most common tools, available from wax manufacturers and many from hardware stores, are:

awl   sharp-pointed steel shaft with a handle, useful in mounting bindings and repairing poles and boots.

bench, waxing   floor-standing or table-mounting stand for holding a ski, base up, for preparation, working, and waxing. Usually, the entire ski is supported, so the bench can sustain heavier work, such as rilling.

brush, hand-held   small, rectangular brushes, with bronze or brass bristle for rilling and preparing bases, and with nylon bristle for finish waxing of rilled bases.

brush, rotary   when fitted to a holder, mounts in an electric drill chuck and is used for removing wax and for rilling Alpine and Telemark skis; several varieties of bristle available.

cork   As the name implies, corks were originally made of natural cork. Synthetic waxing corks, made of expanded plastics, are now more common and smooth wax better than do natural corks. But they also remove more wax from the base, so natural corks are often preferable for fine work.

edge sharpener   a hand-held device, adjustable to any base and side bevels, used for on-hill edge deburring and sharpening.

epoxy glue   for repairing ski and snowboard tops and sides.

file holder   a device, usually of plastic, for holding a file at a set angle, usually 0°, 1°, 1.5°, 2°, 3° or 4°, in filing steel edges of Alpine skis, Telemark skis or snowboards; models for base bevel and side bevel available.

file   similar to a file used in metalworking; of chrome steel, usually with 35 to 50 teeth per inch, used in a file holder to file steel edges.

file, edge   a small, rectangular, single-unit file in a holder made to fit the hand, used for rapid edge filing and sharpening.

groove scraper   a long, thin, usually plastic scraper with its corners formed to fit and scrape wax out of tracking grooves in bases.

hand cleaners   creams that remove wax from hands and clothing; mechanic's waterless hand cleaners also work. Don't use these creams to remove wax from skis or snowboards, as they leave an oily residue that repels wax.

heat gun for warming block-type waxing iron and for warm cleaning of bases. Note: Check voltage before traveling abroad: Japan and the USA have 110 V, while Europe and the rest of the skiing world have 220 V.

horse, waxing like a carpenter's horse, usually made of metal tubing, collapsible for portability; stands free on floor in use and firmly holds one or two skis at a convenient height for preparation, working, and waxing.

iron, block a square block of metal, usually aluminum, fitted with a handle and intended to be heated by a torch.

iron, electric Electric waxing irons resemble household irons, but feature a rectangular sole and a continuously adjustable thermostat more convenient for waxing. Small electric travel irons or household irons can also be used (but not steam irons, as molten wax clogs the nozzles in the sole of the iron). Note: Check voltage before traveling abroad: Japan and the USA have 110 V, while Europe and the rest of the skiing world have 220 V.

kit a case with hinged sections containing compartments for carrying wax and waxing tools; several sizes available, from slightly larger than an attaché case to as large as an overnight suitcase. Some skiers prefer a sturdy metal fishing-tackle box as a wax kit.

polishing stone whetstone used for polishing steel edges; flexible model available for detuning edges at tips and tails.

polyethylene candle a short rod of polyethylene used in base repair, intended to be lit over a base so that molten polyethylene drips down into an area to be filled, usually available in black, blue, and transparent colors.

riller a holder, usually plastic, usually with interchangeable irons of various pitches, used for rilling cross-country ski bases; not used on Alpine or Telemark skis, as they have steel edges.

sanding block a rectangular block, usually with finger grooves on both sides, intended to hold sandpaper used in working on bases.

sandpaper for use on ski bases, usually wrapped around a sanding block; made in cloth- or polyester-backed metal oxide sheets specifically designed for plastics. The grits commonly used in base preparation are #100, #150, #180, #220 and #370, while #60 is used for rubbing the kick zones of classical cross-country skis for waxless grip in slop. Do not use ordinary carpenter's sandpaper on ski bases, as its particles become imbedded in the plastic and slow glide.

scouring pad of nylon, used in preparing and cleaning bases.

scraper Two types are available: pocket scrapers, often in a unit with a cork, for removing wax and scraping bases, and larger steel or plastic scrapers, about the size of a small filing card, used for scraping and repairing bases and for scraping base preparation wax and glide wax. One popular scraper is an ordinary 3 by 5 in. carpenter's refinishing scraper, available in hardware stores. See **groove scraper** and **snowboard scraper**.

screwdriver for driving and tightening binding screws; Pozi-Drive #3 among the most common, but other tips and flutes are used; check your binding instructions to see which.

snowboard scraper an extra-long scraper intended for working on snowboards.

solvents wax-dissolving liquids, available in cans or in pump-spray cans. Biodegradable citrus oil solvent is recommended. Always read all toxicity and flammability warnings on cans before using solvents.

spark lighter as used by welders, a small, hand-held, spring-loaded flint that creates a spark for lighting torches.

ski straps pair of fabric straps with buckles or Velcro closures, or rubber straps with hooks, to hold pair of skis together at tip and tail.

suction cups a frame with two suction cups, similar to those used by glaziers, intended to hold snowboards or jumping skis for preparation, working, or waxing; two types available, with C-clamp for table mount and with shaft for vise mount.

table, waxing a portable, collapsible table, usually about two by four feet and about three feet high, much like a picnic table but far sturdier, for working on skis when no workbench is available.

thermometer Many thermometers can be used to measure the temperature of a snow surface, but the best ones are made specifically for the purpose and have convenient scales in degrees Celsius and Fahrenheit, at practical skiing temperatures. Most are designed to fit in a pocket, and are fitted with a clip or a holder.

torch Used for heating block-type waxing irons; now seldom used for any other purpose, as high flame heats damage bases. The most common types are those fueled by propane cylinders, commonly available in hardware stores, and those fueled by butane cartridges. The propane cylinders are heavier than the butane cartridges for the same amount of gas, but have the advantage that propane burns well down to -30°C (-22°F), while butane freezes at about -1°C (30°F). Caution: gas cylinders are prohibited on passenger aircraft. Also, if you go overseas to ski, leave your torch behind, and borrow or buy one there. European cylinder threads and torch fittings differ from those standardized in the USA.

vises, waxing   pairs of vises, with rubber-lined jaws specifically designed to hold skis; clamped on a workbench.

wiping tissue   Similar to absorbent, lint-free industrial wiping tissue, the tissue offered by wax manufacturers features high absorbency and a surface roughness, and consequently is suited to a variety of waxing tasks, including cleaning, wiping and finish buffing.

Additional items

Wise skiers and snowboarders usually supplement a basic selection of the above tools with a few ordinary items, including:

band-aids and first-aid ointment   primarily for fingers cut or burned.

newspapers   to protect floor from shavings, dust and dribbled wax.

paint brush   for mixing waxes in hot-wax cleaning.

paper towels   to clean up any mess after waxing and to dry hands.

pencil and small pocket notebook   to make notes on waxing and snow conditions; ball-point pens won't do, as they often cease to work when wet or cold.

plastic lunch bags   to put over ski tips and tails when strapping pairs together, or to hold refuse to be discarded elsewhere.

pocket knife   preferably of "Swiss Army" type with many blades, useful for ski repairs as well as for opening bottles for post-race celebrations or wakes.

soap and small hand towel   to wash hands after waxing or cleaning, as even the best of waterless hand cleaners leave the hands slightly oily.

terrycloth toweling or old washcloths   for drying bases and other parts of skis and boards, as before bagging for transport.

TRANSPORTING AND STORING

Clean and protect is the maxim for all transporting and storing all skis and snowboards. Remember, away from snow, they are out of their element and subject to attack from just about everything. **Clean** skis and snowboards before storing them for any extended period (see **Cleaning bases**). Wise skiers and snowboarders finish spring cleaning by warming in a good coating of the glide wax they know will be used the following winter. Then when the first snow falls and they rush to snow, a simple scraping is all that's needed to prepare the bases. Always wipe bindings clean before storing, and follow manufacturer's directions for lubrication, if needed.

Bag skis and snowboards on the road. Carry them in a ski/snowboard bag when traveling, particularly when carrying them on a car roof rack. Road film, exhaust particles, and dust dissolve base plastics. Worse, saltwater, splashed up from salted roads, etches bindings and skis so quickly that you may suspect that the snow sports industry is among those supporting road salting. Best are zippered bags, but the disposable plastic variety that airlines give away free at baggage check-in, or even two overlapped plastic garbage sacks will do. If your car roof rack is of the locking, hinged type intended to carry skis flat, side by side, best swap it for a simpler roof bar and a couple of rubber or shock-cord tie-downs. Toss the bag inside the car if you fear theft when leaving it unattended.

Before bagging, dry and clean a pair of skis and then strap them together, base against base. For extra protection of the bases, place full-width strips of cloth between the bases where they contact behind the ski tips and ahead of the tails. Better yet, use the full-length base protectors available from some wax manufacturers. They slip over tips and are held to bases by several ties along the length of the ski. In a pinch, heavier-gauge plastic lunch bags will do, as they are large enough to slip over tips and tails and reach to the points where the skis contact each other.

Store skis and snowboards in a cool, dry place during off-season. Don't store in an attic, unless it is well insulated and ventilated. Summertime temperatures in an uninsulated, closed attic can be so high that wax on bases melts. This robs the bases of their protective coat of wax. Worse yet, the molten wax can run into messy puddles on the attic floor and down into the underlying insulation, which both degrades it and creates a fire hazard.

TRIBOLOGY

Tribology, the study of friction that includes the scientific theories explaining glide on snow, is a relatively new word. Its prefix "tribo-" comes from the Greek *tribos,* rubbing. The first modern use of the word was in 1917, in *triboelectricity,* the static charge built up on an insulator, as when you run a comb through dry hair and then use it to pick up scraps of paper. The word next appeared in 1950 as *tribophysics,* the scientific principles of friction and lubricants. Finally, in 1960, *tribology* became the term for lubrication technology.

Tribology provides a picture of the reality that is called a *tribological model.* Don't let the "tri" mislead, as it does not mean "three." Four elements are involved: stationary snow, a moving ski or snowboard base, an intervening interface, and the surrounding atmosphere.

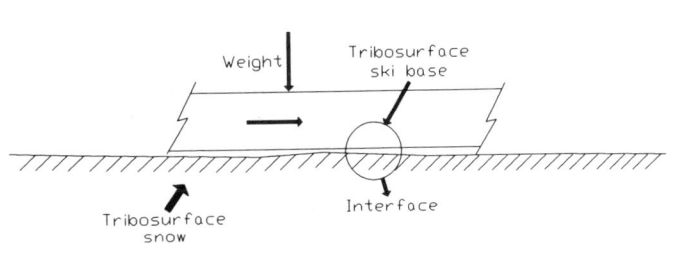

Tribological model consists of four components

A tribological analysis starts by determining a *structure of the system,* which is a description of the materials involved. In glide studies, there are just two materials, each of which may vary. The ski or snowboard base, usually of polyethylene, may be prepared and waxed in many ways. The underlying snow can be in numerous phases and can be natural, packed, treated or artificial, or a combination of these.

The structure of the system sets the stage on which the *operative variables* act. They include the weight of the person on top of the moving base, the speed of the base on the snow, air and snow temperatures, and the duration of glide.

The final analysis is of a *tribological interaction* that takes place in the interface and consequently characterizes it. In turn, knowledge of the nature of the interface aids the design of bases and helps provide guidelines for preparing bases and for choosing and applying waxes.

Tribological analyses are intricate, which is one reason why the first successful results came in the mid 1980s, after computers became commonplace in snow-science laboratories. Though complex for those who design bases and waxes, the essentials of a tribological model of a base-snow interface are plain. A picture of them resembles what you might see if you focused a microscope on the base-to-snow interface as you glide over snow.

The apparently smooth surfaces of the waxed base and the snow underneath it would no longer be smooth. With your imaginary microscope adjusted to view matters at the molecular level, you would see that the two surfaces are both irregular, like a moonscape. Only a few peaks of the two moonscapes would be in contact with each other. This would tell you that only a small percentage of your base actually contacts the snow. The rest of the volume of the interface would be a void, filled with air and water vapor. If the snow was wet, you would also see water. At temperatures around freezing, you would see all these three constituents change rapidly with the smallest changes of temperature, as the entire interface is at the *triple point* of water, when the solid (ice in snow crystals), liquid (free water) and gaseous (water vapor) phases exist simultaneously, in equilibrium with each other. The physics of any material at the triple point is complex, and water is no exception. That's why the challenge of waxing is greatest at temperatures around 0°C (32°F).

Were you to keep your microscope focused on the interface throughout a range of snow conditions, you would see the peaks of the two moonscape surfaces, called *asperites*, mutually deforming, as well as gouging and ripping particles from, each other. That observation would tell you why bases wear with use and why snow in tracks and on slopes becomes worn with use. If you watched carefully to see which surface was the greater offender in this microscopic tussle, you would see the harder of the two surfaces plowing up the softer, just as a farmer's plow turns up earth. You would see the surfaces adhere to each other. You would soon see that the molecular properties of the two surfaces play a complex role along with their mechanical characteristics. This is why your real-world experience and senses can deceive, because waxing for glide on snow has nothing in common with, say, waxing floors or waxing your car. A shine may look nice, but often what counts is the shine which you cannot see with an unaided eye.

But you need not master the intricacies of tribology to benefit from it. Since the early 1990s, ski, snowboard and wax manufacturers have done it for you and have incorporated the results of tribological analyses in their designs. All you need to know is that for ultimate performance, base preparation, wax choice, and wax application are all important in matching the base-snow interface for which products are designed and techniques are recommended.

WAXLESS SKIS

Waxing Waxless

Waxless skis for classical cross-country have mid-base sections that feature mechanical grip, such as grip created by machined or pressed patterns in the base material or inlays of differing materials. Hence the designation "waxless." But experience since they were first introduced in the late 1960s and early 1970s has shown that though waxless skis may be a boon for some recreational skiers (they have infrequently been used in racing) and in ski rental (where the staff has no time to wax for their customers), they are not completely waxless.

First and foremost, waxless skis need cleaning just as do other skis. In fact, they sometimes need more frequent and more thorough cleaning, especially after they have been used on wet snow tracks and have picked up klister that had worn off conventional waxable skis. The klister clogs the waxless grip sections and gradually renders them useless, as well as attracting dirt that can abrade the serrations or imbrications of pattern-type bases. So if you ski on waxless skis, clean them often, using a wax dissolving solvent, a nylon brush and wiping tissue to clean the bases (see **Cleaning bases**).

Second, waxless skis need good glide, just as do waxable skis. In fact, they often need more for the same performance, as the waxless sections frequently drag on snow, which slows glide. So you should glide-wax the tip and tail zones that have no waxless pattern or material (see **Applying wax**).

Finally, just as there is no universal grip wax, there is no waxless grip section that works equally well on all snows. Because grip is fixed by the pattern or material of the grip section, it cannot be altered. But the amount of it can be altered slightly by shortening the effective grip section. Do this by covering shorter areas of it, toward the ski tip and ski tail, with glide wax, as you are glide-waxing the tip and tail zones. Even when length-adjusted, the waxless grip zone may drag on snow. Consequently wax manufacturers offer silicone sprays that enhance the glide of a waxless section.

Rubbing - Made in USA

Waxing for freezing slop - wet, new snow or falling snow mixed with rain, sleet or slush just at freezing - is difficult, as snow characteristics are unstable. Good kick is elusive, and softer waxes and klisters frequently ice up. One workable approach is to rub, or selectively abrade, the base midsections. The abrading raises small polyethylene fibers up from the base. On the right snow conditions, each fiber acts like a small sawtooth, biting into the snow for the grip that gives good kick. Rubbing works only over an extremely narrow range of snow conditions, and it's tough on skis, as some of the base is removed each time it is abraded. But for classical cross-country ski racing in freezing slop, it can be the saving grace of the day. Rubbing is a *Made in USA* technique, originated in 1982 by US Ski Team racers at races in Scandinavia.

Rubbing works best on sintered polyethylene racing ski bases. Extruded plastic bases, common on recreational skis, black polyethylene (graphite doped) bases, and some cross-linked polyethylene bases perform poorly when rubbed. Skis to be rubbed should have a camber slightly stiffer than a dry-snow, or "powder" camber but not quite as stiff as a wet-snow "klister" camber. Few racers enjoy the luxury of setting aside a pair of skis dedicated to rubbing, so most use an old pair of klister skis.

Start rubbing with a ski firmly fixed in a waxing horse or vises, base up, and completely clean. You may glide-wax the tip and tail zones before or after rubbing. Rub with coarse sandpaper wrapped around a sanding block. Use a coarser grit, #60, for rougher rubbing of skis to be used in tracks that pack and polish to a glaze. Use a finer grit, #160, for smoother rubbing of skis to be used in continuously falling new snow and slop.

Rub the **kick zone** of a ski much as you would sand it to improve wax adhesion, but rub in the tip-to-tail direction only, over a length equal to that where you normally would apply wet-snow klister, about 14 to 18 in. Rub until the kick zone looks as if it were made of fine fur. When in doubt, rub too little rather than too much, as excessive rubbing slows glide.

Follow rubbing by brushing and wiping off all polyethylene dust. Raw rubbed kick zones on bases will ice up if the skis are used directly. So the rubbed zones must be protected. Wax manufacturers offer silicone sprays for the purpose. Spray the liquid on the rubbed kick zones, and let the skis stand until completely dry. Top racers now prefer dry application of fluorocarbon powder in the rub, as it's more durable than silicone spray and needs no drying time.

Like factory-made waxless ski bases, do-it-yourself rubbed bases are a fixed, mechanical approach to grip. Once on skis, you cannot change grip without going back into the wax room to redo the job. So always try rubbing in training, to gain experience with it, before using it in racing.

WORDS

English-speaking skiers and snowboarders occasionally lament a linguistic disadvantage compared to speakers of other languages, which have richer vocabularies for describing snow and waxing. Eskimos, for instance, are said to have 400 words for snow. Such ostensible advantages are arguable.

In *The Language Instinct*, (New York, William Morrow, 1994, ISBN 0-688-12141-1, and London, Penguin, 1994, ISBN 0-713-9099-6), Steven Pinker, a professor of cognitive science at MIT, debunks the Eskimo vocabulary hoax. He points out (p. 64) that Eskimos "do not have four hundred words for snow, as it has been claimed in print, or two hundred, or one hundred, or forty-eight, or even nine. One dictionary puts the figure at two." Haphazard linguistic research started the story; exaggeration inflated it.

Likewise, the Scandinavian languages and German are held to be more precise in describing snow and more varied in describing waxing. That view, too, is inflated, though not as much as the Eskimo vocabulary hoax. The international vocabulary of glaciology, which includes snows, has been incorporated in English. A mountaineer recognizes *névé* and *firn*, both in the Random House Dictionary of the English Language, as precise, synonymous terms for the granular snow that accumulates and compacts to become glacial ice. Translations of the terms of the international vocabulary of glaciology into other languages occasionally creep back into the English jargon of snow sports, usually because the original translators of directions for waxes didn't know the words in English. Norway, where a lot of wax is produced and where this book was written, has been one source of translated-term feedback. Examples include two Norwegian terms for snow, *skare* (crust) and *fokk* (windpack).

However, for waxes, there are two borderline exceptions. In contradistinction to the Scandinavian languages, English fails to differentiate between wax, the generic term for a large group of fatty solids, and the variety of wax that you put on your skis or snowboard, which, in some cases, may contain no wax at all. Norwegian, for instance, solves the problem neatly, as *voks* (wax) is reserved for compounds made primarily of waxes, while *skismöring* (ski lubricant) applies to the products used on ski and snowboard bases. *Skismöring* seems as unlikely to catch on in English as does its translation, "ski lubricant."

English is often said to lack a native word for the sticky paste that classical cross-country skiers use for grip on wetter and older snows, while Norwegian has the specific term *klister* (sticky paste). That's a half truth. The Norwegian word came via Swedish from the German *Kleister*. It was first used to describe a ski wax in 1913, when Peter Östbye so named the paste-like wax he had invented for grip and glide on wet snows. According to the second unabridged edition of The Random House Dictionary of the English Language, *klister* has been used in English since the late 1930s. The complete second edition of The Oxford English Dictionary states a more specific date, 1936. So that puts English just 23 years behind Norwegian in accepting a German word that is now used throughout the world of snow sports.

Index